A 101 Action Research Guide for Beginners

A 101 Action Research Guide for Beginners

Demystifying Research Terminology using A Concrete STEM Action Research Project

Saba Ahmed

PETER LANG
Oxford · Berlin · Bruxelles · Chennai · Lausanne · New York

Bibliographic information published by the Deutsche Nationalbibliothek.
The German National Library lists this publication in the German
National Bibliography; detailed bibliographic data is available on the Internet
at http://dnb.d-nb.de.

A catalogue record for this book is available from the British Library.

Library of Congress Cataloging-in-Publication Data

Names: Ahmed, Saba, 1987- author.
Title: A 101 action research guide for beginners : demystifying research
   terminology using a concrete STEM action research project / Saba Ahmed.
Other titles: One hundred and one action research guide for beginners
Description: New York : Peter Lang, [2024] | Includes bibliographical
   references.
Identifiers: LCCN 2024024559 (print) | LCCN 2024024560 (ebook) |
   ISBN 9781803745824 (paperback) | ISBN 9781803745831 (ebook) |
   ISBN 9781803745848 (epub)
Subjects: LCSH: Action research in education. | Research—Terminology. |
   Science—Study and teaching. | Technology—Study and teaching.
Classification: LCC LB1028.24 .A43 2024 (print) | LCC LB1028.24 (ebook) |
   DDC 370.72—dc23/eng/20240601
LC record available at https://lccn.loc.gov/2024024559
LC ebook record available at https://lccn.loc.gov/2024024560

Cover design by Peter Lang Group AG

ISBN 978-1-80374-582-4 (print)
ISBN 978-1-80374-583-1 (ePDF)
ISBN 978-1-80374-584-8 (ePub)
DOI 10.3726/b22030

© 2024 Peter Lang Group AG, Lausanne
Published by Peter Lang Ltd, Oxford, United Kingdom
info@peterlang.com - www.peterlang.com

Saba Ahmed has asserted her right under the Copyright, Designs and Patents Act, 1988,
to be identified as Author of this Work.

All rights reserved.
All parts of this publication are protected by copyright.
Any utilisation outside the strict limits of the copyright law, without the permission of the
publisher, is forbidden and liable to prosecution.
This applies in particular to reproductions, translations, microfilming, and storage and
processing in electronic retrieval systems.

This publication has been peer reviewed.

Contents

List of Figures and Tables — vii

Acknowledgements — ix

Introduction — 1

CHAPTER 1
Contemporary STEM Teaching — 17

CHAPTER 2
Tips for Academic and Reflective Writing — 27

CHAPTER 3
Demystifying Basic Research Terminology — 43

CHAPTER 4
An Introduction to Data Collation Methods — 53

CHAPTER 5
Maintaining Quality Assurance — 61

CHAPTER 6
An Example of a Research Proposal — 69

CHAPTER 7
An Exemplar STEM Lecturer Action Research Project — 83

CHAPTER 8
The Virtues of Developing the Grassroots Researcher/Action Researcher for future STEM Practice   111

Afterword   119

Appendix 1: Academic Writing/Harvard Referencing Tasks 1 & 2 Plan (Free Resource)   121

Appendix 2: TES Article How to Improve College Students' Academic Writing   127

Appendix 3: HEA Fellowship Application Reflective Account   129

Appendix 4: ITTECF   143

Appendix 5: ETF Professional Standards for Teachers and Trainers   145

Appendix 6: Global Framework of Professional Teaching Standards from the Joint EI/UNESCO   147

List of Figures and Tables

Figure 1	Microbiology Multiple Choice Questions Task	9
Figure 2	UTI Case Study Task	10
Figure 3	Impact Journal Image on Lenses	31
Figure 4	Learning Analytics Student Reflective Accounts Data	94
Figure 5	Examples of Student Reflective Accounts Comments	96
Figure 6	Lecturer Questionnaire Data for the Moodle Academic Writing Skills/Harvard Referencing Task	101
Figure 7	Lecturer comments on the Moodle Academic Writing/Harvard Referencing Skills Task	102
Figure 8	Lecturer Responses for the Remaining Questions on the Lecturer Questionnaires	103
Table 1	Results on Student Reflective Accounts	95
Table 2	A Table to Show Student Feedback on How the Microbiology Lesson Could Be Further Improved	133

Acknowledgements

This book is dedicated to my family and friends who have been incredibly supportive in my journey as a lecturer and as an author. To all of those who have provided advice along the way I am immensely grateful. I want to highlight that the completion of this book and my career opportunities to date would not have been possible without support from my peers and my department leads Shelley Mannion and Gail Holmes.

Introduction

The main premise of the book is to demystify research terminology for those teaching and completing action research projects. Research terms such as systematic reviews, meta-analysis, primary research, and literature reviews will be explained in a simple manner with solid links to practice put across. Personally, I found research terminology hard to decipher after such a long gap (almost a decade) between completing my dissertation at undergraduate level, and then having to do an action research project for my postgraduate diploma. This book is written for all researchers in the same position.

In Chapter 1 contemporary STEM (Science, Technology, Engineering and Mathematics) teaching examples, and teacher roles and responsibilities will be explored alongside current societal issues. Ongoing commentary on how teaching experiences, reflection, and how current theory can be used to inform action research projects to achieve real-world benefits will be discussed. The second chapter presents a strong foundation on differences between academic writing and reflective writing. In Chapters 3 and 4 research terminology, and common data collation methods are examined. Chapter 5 provides coverage on the importance of quality assurance.

An example research proposal is presented in Chapter 6, and the action research project report in its entirety is included in Chapter 7. The report in Chapter 7 contains the following:

- abstract
- contents page
- introduction/rationale/background with clear aims and objectives
- literature review
- methodology
- results/results discussion
- conclusion/recommendations
- references
- appendices

By sharing the report in full readers of the book can gauge how local research is immensely valuable in education settings, to elevate levels of student achievement. The example action research project depicts how quality assurance was routinely instilled throughout the project.

In the final chapter it promotes the noteworthiness of growing researcher skillsets at undergraduate level, therefore future STEM graduates are equipped with the tools to be able to conduct impactful local/action research in their future practice. Teaching provision on courses with research project modules should never be disconnected with practice. The chapters in the book signify the wins that can be gained from action research/local research using real-life examples and highlight what to watch out for in terms of potential obstacles that could be encountered in research projects.

The main terms related to action research will be set out in the introduction, and this provides a foundation appreciation on action research. The different parts of the short guide connect action research with national and international frameworks in teaching and make links with wider key research principles.

Action Research

Action research is about applying an action or actions to resolve an issue identified at the same time as researching it. First-person, second-person, and third-person action research are outlined next:

- First-person action research within teaching is where the researcher engages in research to ascertain deeper insight into own inquiry to see how to improve teaching pedagogy. It may be useful in trying out a hunch on a small scale to test whether it has any legs and is an independent form of research.
- Second-person action research differs from the first-person route, where action research is conducted collaboratively in small groups on an issue identified to garner positive increments. It could be that there is a shared issue that requires attention in a teaching department to improve learner attainment levels, so a joint effort is more beneficial. They are both actors and researchers in the action research project. Elements of the first-person and second-person action research approaches were used in the action research project in Chapter 7.

- Third-person action research is completed on a bigger scale and is done in large groups, where the research could be carried out across different education organisations. It could be used to research a particular concern to improve it through interventions. Action research could start off in the first-person then traverse to the second-person route, and in the next research cycle it may expand into third-person action research. (Hartney, 2020)

The two main types of action research are participatory action research and practical action research. Participatory action research asserts that those taking part in the research should be members of the community that are in the study, and they should be encouraged to participate and share their experiences (in essence being co-researchers) (Cutting, n.d.). The second type is practical action research, which is where the design and methodology in the research are more attuned to addressing and coming up with solutions for the area of concern.

Action research has overlapping features with scholarship of teaching and learning (SoTL) research, where action research could be used as a methodological approach in SoTL-based research projects. Analysis of research, working with peers and critical reflection are fundamentals to the SoTL approach. It is becoming more commonplace for teachers to critically reflect then draw on published evidence, and undertake research to acquire gains in teaching practice on areas such as curriculum development and learner provision. Lecturers and teachers can then make positive contributions to build on existing literature in the area that they are researching, and share valuable findings with others (The University of Edinburgh, 2024). Although sometimes there can be a disconnect between teacher action research and enhancing skills for learners to use in their future STEM practice.

Ways of Aligning Action Research to Government Frameworks

The new Initial Teacher Training and Early Career Framework (ITTECF) framework strongly backs reflective conversations between those new to teaching and their mentors, and in accessing support from experienced teaching professionals. If there is a behavioural issue, then troubleshoot how interventions and tactics can be utilised to overcome this with colleagues. Having these peer discussions can be vital in shaping solutions to issues faced within local educational settings, and perhaps inform research proposals for teacher practitioners undertaking action research projects to develop areas that need modifications, to improve learner outcomes on the problem area discovered (DFE, 2024). With the topic areas being researched cogitate how any marked improvements can be assessed in a qualitative/quantitative manner (these terms will be covered in greater depth in Chapters 3 and 4). It is one way where the use of action research, and in particular the use of second-person action research could be extremely useful to help improve an area in teaching. Again, if the first cycle of intervention/interventions does not lead to desired changes then work together with the teaching team, and reflect through the peer, autobiographical, theoretical and student perspectives in the Brookfield's lenses to assess how this could be furthered. This is an example of a reflective model, which is covered in Chapter 2.

Each action research project and teacher practitioner research project will be unique, and therefore a different methodology and research project design could be more suitable. By furnishing an overview of research terminology it will aid researchers in measuring the quality of published literature, and evidence-based research out there. Bear in mind that not all research is of the same quality. There is a hierarchy to published data.

Next to be expressed are the different learning theories those new to teaching will come across. Learning theories can significantly impact interventions implemented by teachers (new or experienced) in action research projects, therefore a quick summary of key elements related to learning theories will be useful for readers of the book. Like all embarking on a new career, I was struck with periods of enthusiasm, embracing the unknown with an open mind interspersed with times of doubt. I often pondered, how can the theory I am coming across be employed in a substantial way to improve student attainment levels and the learner journey? I felt like "what the heck are the … gogies" and felt overloaded with too many ... "isms". Possibly a sentiment shared with many readers of the book.

All educators new to teaching will be exposed to many "...isms" (behaviourism, humanism, constructivism, cognitivism) where teachers will be confronted with unravelling how theories are consequential in course delivery, to improve the learner experience and their teaching pedagogy. Each teacher is different, and the pertinence of each learning theory will differ. Some may find humanism elements more useful, and yet others may favour constructivism (this is to be expected). Yet all teachers need to demonstrate an understanding and openness to other learning theories, because unexpectedly it could add value if not now then potentially in future practice. Teaching practice is a spectrum. By learning the foundations of each theory teachers/lecturers can pick and choose the level and degree to which it permeates into their teaching delivery, and on how they can affect action research projects. After experimenting if these prove unsuccessful, then don't be dejected. It all still counts as a learning experience.

Pedagogy, Andragogy and Heutagogy

There are three main "...gogies" in education. These being pedagogy, andragogy and heutagogy. They sound like alien concepts but show how teaching styles can vary. Pedagogy is how the teacher delivers the curriculum (Peel, 2024). In essence it is the culmination of how the background of a teacher their experiences, and how other factors such as feedback from observations, and the applications of learning theories influences their practice. It is ever evolving and could be critical to the first-person action research route.

Andragogy on the other hand sees "self-directed learning" being centre stage, and it can assist students, especially in healthcare settings with lifelong learning. Many healthcare professionals must undertake yearly continuing professional development (CPD), and revalidation. Andragogy is linked to teaching adults, and it favours self-directed learning with teachers acting as facilitators (Knowles, 1975).

Influential writers such as Blashke and Hase (2016) support heutagogy principles. This concept describes how students use key skills and reflection to steer their own "self-determined learning". Here students are encouraged to comprehend how they best learn, which again is critical in the CPD component for the lifelong learning of healthcare and STEM professionals. Some teacher/lecturer action research projects may be focused on using these concepts to encourage reflective practice growth in their students. This is considered in the action research project in Chapter 7.

Learning Theories & STEM Education

Within this section the many "…isms" and learning theories teachers/lecturers new to the profession are being exposed to will be reviewed, with concrete examples from own STEM teaching practice on pharmacy courses. These learning theories could feed into the teaching pedagogy of readers of the book and assist them to come up with a novel approach to facilitate an improvement in the curriculum delivery in their own action research projects. Don't be afraid to try something new and if it didn't prove as successful as anticipated the first time around, then teaching strategies can be adapted to see how it could become more prosperous for the next time. The way learning theories influence each teacher/lecturer in practice will depend on their experience, their students, and the subjects they are teaching.

These learning theories include:

- Behaviourism
- Cognitivism
- Constructivism
- Humanism
- Social Learning Theory
- Situated Learning Theory

Behaviourism

In this learning theory it is summed up as learning being transmitted to the students from the teacher, and the learner commits this to memory. Using positive stimulus this is reinforced and learning is achieved. The delivery is teacher-dominated and students are viewed as blank slates (tabula rasa). Notable writers purporting behaviourism include:

- Pavlov (who was behind the famous experiment where upon ringing a bell, this elicited the dogs to salivate in anticipation of food, that is, the stimulus to shore up learning).
- Skinner who claimed that learning was an outcome of operant conditioning.
- Thorndike

Thorndike's law of effect is defined as:

> Of several responses made to the same situation those which are accompanied or closely followed by satisfaction to the animal will, other things being equal, be more firmly connected with the situation, so that, when it recurs, they will be more likely to recur ... the greater the satisfaction, the greater the strengthening .... (Thorndike, 1911 as cited by Beeler, 2012)

There has been research conducted on the link between the dopamine reward pathway, and instructional learning albeit on mice. The data showed that greater levels of dopamine reduced thriftiness and encouraged wider exploration using more energy expenditure. On the other hand, lower dopamine levels exhibited more thriftiness and favoured the exploitation of prior reward learning, and diminished exploration of areas.

Operant conditioning is a learning approach where repetition is associated with the outcomes of the response. In short anything which is positively rewarded will be repeated, but anything which is punished will not be repeated. An example which could be used to understand operant conditioning is smoking, that continues after initiation due to the rapid positive impact of nicotine on the dopamine reward system. Nicotine, which is the addictive active ingredient in smoking acts on the brain to cause an increment in dopamine levels, which triggers a mild euphoric action. This dopamine surge serves as a positive stimulus to continue with the behaviour. In those that have a negative effect from the first or early exposure to a stimulus, it means that they will be less likely to continue with it (Beeler, 2012).

Most educators will argue that behaviourist learning tactics on their own will not elucidate meaningful learning. Although some behaviourist methods such as commending someone on a brilliant answer to a question posed is important to bolster positive behaviour and learning. Other teachers may employ behaviourist strategies such as changing their body language, and crossing their arms if the class becomes too unsettled. The students learn from repeated experience that the lecturer is waiting for them to quieten down before continuing with the lesson.

Cognitivism

In the realms of cognitivism, the learner is observed as having more input in comparison to classical behaviourism. There is a shift away from traditional behaviourism theories and the blank slate concept. The students are viewed as being able to disseminate and find meaning in the concepts that they are learning, rather than learning as an outcome of a stimulus. Students internally process the learning content and learning is seen as a change in knowledge, which is committed to memory as opposed to a transformation in behaviour as theorised in behaviourism. Bruner (n.d., cited in Johnston 2012) was a strong proponent of cognitivism and used the concept of "the spiral curriculum". Key topics were repeatedly visited throughout the entire course delivery. In essence learning from another unit was revisited in a different unit to help students make connections (build schema) and realise a deeper level of understanding with more complex learning. Revisiting key concepts in different units can strengthen learning from previous units.

1.Bacteria have larger ribosomes than mammalian cells? Single choice.
(1/1 Point)
- ☐ True
- ☐ False

2.Out of the following antibiotics which targets the ribosomes of bacteria? Single choice.
(1/1 Point)
- ☐ Amoxicillin
- ☐ Cefalexin
- ☐ Clarithromycin
- ☐ Vancomycin

Figure 1. Microbiology Multiple Choice Questions Task

A practical example of using the concept of the spiral curriculum in own teaching practice was to repeatedly reexamine key concepts on proteins from the first unit, biology and then again in the next unit microbiology. This connected the learning on both modules. When the lecturer was covering the mechanism of action of antibiotics on targeting the smaller ribosomes in bacteria in contrast to larger ribosomes in animal cells (ribosomes are the key cell organelle which manufacture proteins), they were able to use the concept of the spiral curriculum to fortify learning. It was a useful tactic to relay across how learning about proteins, and cellular differences between bacterial and animal cells were central to understanding the modes of action for the various antibiotic classes, and different drug targets for antibiotics. See above an example of quiz questions set for the online students to help accomplish this.

Constructivism

For constructivism this builds on prior knowledge to create more tangible links between different areas being studied (Scales, 2008). Reflection and

At your place of work, you receive a prescription for trimethoprim 200mg bd for three days for a 34 year old pregnant female pregnant who is in her first trimester

Q1) Comment on the suitability of this prescription for this patient?

Q2) Looking at your local guidelines what would be first line treatment, and what would be the course length duration?

Q3) Provide an overview of the diagnostic tests in UTI management, and explain the rationale behind them?

Q4) Research what is the most common causative pathogen associated in UTIs?

Figure 2. UTI Case Study Task

analysis are strongly backed in this educational approach to teaching. In this theory the students are more active in their learning and are observed as information sifters and constructers. Problem-based learning, research and group work are at the pinnacle of designing learning tasks that are constructivist in nature.

Figure 2 (above) is a formative assessment (a case study) created by the lecturer/teacher. It was based on treating a urinary tract infection (UTI) and has constructivist dimensions.

In this task the case study devised tested the students' problem-solving abilities to analyse local protocols from their NHS trusts to come up with an alternative that was safer to use in treating a UTI in the first trimester of pregnancy, and to broaden their awareness of diagnostic tests used. A constructivist approach to formative assessment design, and curriculum delivery can be used in teaching practice to hone the problem-solving and analytical skills for students from different disciplines. Readers of the book will most likely use learning theories/a mixture of learning theories in their interventions for improving an area in their action research projects.

Humanism

In humanism the student is more active and prominent in the learning techniques, which contrasts with behaviourism where students are discerned as empty receptacles to take in information. Learners are viewed as passive in the latter. With humanism it posits that the student oversees their learning and possesses intrinsic motivation to learn. The student voice is encouraged, and a platform should be provided for them to dynamically take part in their learning. This is a shared facet in constructivism. With the teacher being a facilitator rather than the autocratic teacher conveyed in behaviourism. Notable writers for humanism include Maslow and Rodgers.

One of the key examples demonstrating a humanistic approach to formative assessment task design from own experience is the Academic Writing/Harvard referencing tasks created for both courses (included in Appendix 1). This was developed to get the students accustomed to assignment writing. By allowing students to be introduced to academic writing at the course induction without the high levels of stress attached to summative assignments, it can help to reduce the apprehension linked with academic writing for summative assessments. This is because they have already been able to demonstrate academic writing proficiency with a low stakes piece of work (Rogers, 1983, cited in Gravells, 2014, p. 45). The students receive personalised feedback on where they can enhance in these areas. This is completed on both courses at the induction stage to encourage academic writing skills growth, right from the start of their higher education course. The task has both constructivist and humanistic leanings and was part of the action research project included in Chapter 7.

Social Learning Theory

Social learning theory is advocated by Bandura (n.d., cited in Pajares 2002) and is likened as the bridge between traditional behaviourism and the cognitive approach. It encompasses that learning occurs through observing others, imitating and from modelling. On the courses discussed, the students have workplace mentors, and senior colleagues who serve as expert witnesses in their organisation. It is a theory which holds many plusses for student apprentices.

Extending this further it is where social learning theory comes to pole position within teaching in own specialism, as each trainee pharmacy technician has a workplace mentor. They shadow other senior members of staff which exemplifies vicarious learning (Pajares, 2002). This is imperative for trainees as they need to have a professional role model who embodies the GPhC (General Pharmaceutical Council) professional standards and exhibits best practice in their work therefore the student acquires key skills. With any profession however, there are individuals who are "bad apples". They may display bad practice, so again this needs to be factored in. It can be a real concern, because this may lead to the students picking up potentially dangerous practice.

Situated Learning Theory

Another key learning theory is situated learning theory (SLT) and Lave is an influential proponent for this learning theory. This theory proposes that learning occurs as an interaction between the apprentice on the periphery with experts in the field, to then hopefully hold the mantle of "expert" themselves one day (Scales, 2008). Here communities of practice are created, and this theory overlaps with other theories such as social learning theory, cognitivism, and constructivism. Concepts such as the "more knowledgeable other", which are central to learning in constructivism, have overlapped with SLT. The students on the BTEC level 4 course have a Telegram group, which serves as a digital community of practice. In the live Microsoft Teams lessons, breakout rooms are created for students to work through case study questions in groups. This polishes problem-solving and teamworking skills for the students. It has the added benefit of helping to overcome the isolation from studying on remote courses.

By having an open approach and using multiple learning theories in curriculum delivery (e.g. with creating formative and summative assessments), it brings key topics to life. It varies the learning content to engage learners and helps make the course delivery more inclusive. Learning theories can be applied in different ways in action research projects to see if they can generate improvements in learning provision.

The Untapped Potential of Action Research

There is huge scope in the use of action research/local research projects to generate genuine benefits in an area of concern in education settings, and this should be backed by published research. Secondary research should be reflected on to acquire the theoretical perspective. Action research is a prized tool in developing future educators (potentially aiding teacher retention), and in improving learner provision. It can support the students they are teaching with acquiring foundation skills useful to their future careers or help foster deeper learning for complex concepts through researching and testing new strategies (especially when combined with newer concepts and the main learning theories summarised). In FE settings action research is lacking especially within the UK, and more of this is necessary to improve student attainment levels. Within regional networks good practice can be shared, to uplift the practice of other educators.

Conducting local or action research projects in STEM teaching disciplines with collaborative, and reflective elements buttressed with relevant theory provides legitimacy to novel interventions made in teaching practice. Moreover, by possessing a comprehensive understanding on how research principles translate into STEM fields to revolutionise, and improve areas is integral for teaching on courses where students need to complete research projects. This will succour researcher skillsets in students enrolled on these types of courses, which will be essential for their future STEM practice.

Each action research project and teacher practitioner research project will be unique, and therefore a different methodology and research project design could be more suitable. Bear in mind that not all research is of the same quality. There is a hierarchy to published data.

The themes set out in the introduction will be scrutinised repeatedly in the remaining chapters in this short guide. Good luck to all with your research projects. I hope that the book unveils insight into the profoundness of research in addressing a specific concern that may be observed in practice, to improve an area that is lacking for all up-and-coming researchers. For those ECTs (early career teachers) or established expert teacher practitioners in education conducting research the book will serve as a useful manual with contemporary practical examples to make research terminology and concepts clearer. It is written in a relatable and practical manner to make this more accessible for anyone doing action research projects especially for STEM teacher practitioners. This 101 action research guide will enable a firm foundation on elementary research principles to be established for those undertaking action research projects.

A free quiz can be accessed by readers of the book to test their knowledge, by using a Smartphone to scan the following QR code or the readers can click the link below:

<https://forms.office.com/e/2gK6fWQ2wF?origin=lprLink>

Bibliography

Beeler, J. A. (2012) *Thorndike's Law 2.0: Dopamine and the Regulation of Thrift*. [Online] Available from: <https://www.frontiersin.org/articles/10.3389/fnins.2012.00116/full>. [Accessed 22 October 2022].

Blashke, L. M., and Hase, S. (2016). Chapter 2: A Holistic Framework for Creating Twenty-First Century Self-Determined Learners. In B. Gros, Kinshuk., & M. Maina (eds), *The Future of Ubiquitous Learning Designs for Emerging Pedagogies*. Berlin: Springer-Verlag, pp. 25–40.

Cutting, K. (n.d.) *Participatory Action Research*. [Online] Available from: <https://research.ncl.ac.uk/methodshub/methods/participatoryactionresearch/>. [Accessed 13 January 2024].

Department for Education. (2024) *Initial Teacher Training and Early Career Framework*. [Online] Available from: <https://assets.publishing.service.gov.uk/media/65b8fa60e9e10a00130310b2/Initial_teacher_training_and_early_career_framework_30_Jan_2024.pdf>. [Accessed 24 March 2024].

Gravells, A. (2014) *The Award in Education and Training*. London: SAGE.

Hartney, E. (2020) *Action Research in the midst of COVID-19*. [Online] Available from: <https://www.royalroads.ca/sls/action-research-midst-covid-19>. [Accessed 07 March 2024].

Johnston, H. (2012) *The Spiral Curriculum*. [Online] Available from: <https://files.eric.ed.gov/fulltext/ED538282.pdf>. [Accessed 02 November 2022].

Knowles, M. S. (1975) *Self-Directed Learning. A guide for learners and teachers*. Englewood Cliffs: Prentice Hall/Cambridge.

Pajares, F. (2002) *Overview of social cognitive theory and of self-efficacy*. [Online] Available from: <https://people.wku.edu/richard.miller/banduratheory.pdf>. [Accessed 22 October 2022].

Peel, E. A. (2024) *History & Society pedagogy*. [Online] Available from: <https://www.britannica.com/science/pedagogy>. [Accessed 17 March 2024].

Scales, P. (2008) *Teaching in the Lifelong Learning Sector*. Maidenhead: Open University Press.

The University of Edinburgh. (2024) *Scholarship of Teaching and Learning (SOTL)*. [Online] Available from: <https://institute-academic-development.ed.ac.uk/learning-teaching/staff/sotl> [Accessed 26 August 2024].

CHAPTER 1

Contemporary STEM Teaching

Introduction

Teaching at times can take place in a vacuum where societal issues are not probed, and taught content can become too abstract without connections formed with current practice or with the world of work. For teaching on STEM courses, it is necessary to maintain those integral links with practice. This will be the focus of this chapter, alongside teacher roles and responsibilities. The importance of reflective practice in teaching will be illustrated in Chapter 2.

Current Backdrop for Teaching & Contemporary Issues Impacting the Teaching Workforce

A recent NEU (National Education Union) survey showcases how burnout, and issues cited such as unmanageable workloads with increasing leadership duties without having enough time to effectively carry out these extra responsibilities, as the primary reasons being verbalised by teachers on why they may quit the profession and take strike action. In addition, lower wages compared to other countries is another reason why many new teachers may move abroad or are contemplating this. This mirrors other fields, where doctors, nurses and engineers may wish to move away from the UK after qualifying to seek a better quality of life and better wages.

All these reasons have been compounded more so by the pandemic pressures on teaching, and other sectors with the uncertainty over lockdowns coupled with the "cost-of-living crisis" everyone is enduring. This may mean potentially a vast portion of the workforce could leave the teaching profession in the UK worsening the current climate for teaching, and specifically exacerbate the scarcity of STEM (Science, Technology, Engineering and Mathematics) teachers (Guardian News and Media Limited, 2022). Adequate remuneration packages with a structured and supported pathway for local research and action research for teaching staff (early career teachers, and for experienced teachers alike) could be one useful way to maintain and fill the gaps in teaching vacancies. Having a mechanism in place to identify the gaps in resources and improve learning through researching local interventions could alleviate some issues on the ground level for teaching staff in their classrooms. This reflects some of the aspects of the SoTL approach mentioned previously. The reasons for high levels of vacancies in all sectors in teaching is multifactorial, and a multipronged approach is best to help with supporting the retention of teachers and educators in these fields.

Other Issues Impacting Teaching

The demands for mental health services are on the rise due to, but not confined to factors such as the pandemic pressures, personal circumstances, and the cost-of-living crisis (there are numerous other reasons). These are just some of the underlying reasons. Being in the know of where support services can be accessed is paramount.

Society is still reeling from the aftershocks of lockdowns especially in younger age groups in all disciplines causing an upsurge in mental health disorders. One startling statistic is that roughly 33 per cent of 16–24-year-olds experienced some form of depression or anxiety (MIND, 2023). Social isolation could have been a major contributory factor for this rise observed.

These could be some of the pertinent issues that students are facing in educational establishments. Setting high standards of teaching with appropriate novel interventions to support students can be lifechanging for all students, especially disadvantaged children in terms of acquiring good quality education to facilitate career opportunities as stipulated in standard 1 of the DFE Teachers' Standards, and principle 3 in the joint EI/UNESCO framework (see appendices 4 and 6 respectively) (Department for Education, 2024; Education International and UNESCO, 2022).

Teacher Roles and Responsibilities

Holtrop (1997) suggests that "obviously teachers wear many hats friend, counsellor, judge, mentor ….", which resonates strongly with many in the profession as they attempt to sum up the multiple modalities and responsibilities of a teacher. What is key is finding the balance on how much can be dealt through own competence, and when a referral may be necessary. Sometimes the issue may be outside of the teachers' scope to deal with. Teachers need to appreciate that they are not an island and come to terms with not being able to deal with all situations they encounter. This is a key duty for a teacher to come to terms with. Consequently, they should make themselves aware of student support facilities (financial or counselling). For any safeguarding concerns, teachers need to liaise with the relevant team in their organisation to support the student (Gravells, 2014). If there is an immediate risk to the safety of the student or to the public, then the police need to be contacted.

Honing Soft Skills in Learners

The roles and responsibilities of a teacher are wide-ranging. The wider outlook on what students will accomplish, and skills taken away or refined on a course to aid career opportunities should be a priority too. This may engender better outcomes for students on STEM courses, through a broader focus on nurturing generic workplace skills. Careers are fluid, therefore building up this generic skillset is essential. Literacy, analytical, and problem-solving skills development, and IT skills can be deficient at times on STEM courses. Engraining these into courses aids key skills development to support career opportunities, and may encourage retention of future STEM workers, because they have the necessary skills to prosper in their future careers.

Using Artificial Intelligence (AI) in Teaching

The rise in artificial intelligence (AI) in various fields including STEM areas could lead to an over-reliance on AI. This could be counterproductive to wider generic workplace skills advancement. In turn creating a future workforce that is less creative with less developed analytical research skills, and weaker problem-solving capabilities.

The appropriate and well-targeted use of AI, however, could be extremely favourable if done so with the intent of improving time availability for professionals in their field to scan for issues, and use critical analysis skills to solve issues identified. If the AI technology was able to complete the time-consuming tasks such as paperwork, data input etc., then it could mean more time being available for tasks that require greater cognitive input from professionals. For teachers it could assist with marking formative assessments. This could free up time for teachers to support students and have more time available to come up with more creative learning strategies consequently refining different skillsets in their students.

On the other hand, if students start to use AI systems such as ChatGPT (one of many AI systems) or professionals use it in their settings inappropriately, then it may lead to mishaps or a contraction of critical analysis skills within these workforces. Could it lead to incorrect information being cited? Or incorrect learning taking place? Incorrect information could be cascaded to others inadvertently if the information was automatically deemed as reliable without verifying it. Using AI to perform tasks requiring critical analysis without checking the credibility of it could have negative consequences, such as others in the profession being misinformed.

One such case where two lawyers in America used ChatGPT to research a legal case they were representing led to improper information being used as a citation, which turned out to include false cases in an aviation injury claim (Milmo and agency, 2023). They were fined and it most likely had negative ramifications on their reputations as lawyers, which reinforces the notion that there should be apt and careful use of AI in different fields. These critical analysis skills need to be progressed in educational settings, especially in further education and higher education institutions, because they will be essential in producing a future workforce equipped to carry out their professional roles and responsibilities.

Critical analytical skills can be developed solidly in independent research projects/action research projects completed locally by students. When teachers have strong researcher skills, then this can be advantageous in raising these skills in students too. Lecturers and educators that encourage students to authenticate information they research in their studies, supports those learners in their future careers to fact check information to reduce error. It advocates the apt use of AI in future practice and not to use it blindly when conducting research or action research. These are some dilemmas and aspects which need safeguards to be incorporated into the application of AI systems in different fields including education. It is paramount that critical research skills, and literacy skills development for students in STEM disciplines and other fields alike are not neglected.

The use of AI in teaching materials needs to be checked by the teacher to guarantee that taught content is accurate and used in a manner to hone wider skills. There is potential for AI systems to be exploited positively, to create dynamic learning environments leading to soft skills enhancements, and to promote deeper learning.

Use of Contemporary Teaching Approaches

In this section examples from teaching on pharmacy courses will be drawn on. It is a STEM field, where students cover modules on pharmacology, microbiology, patient monitoring and healthcare. In the past differentiation was used more in teaching. Differentiation is related to teaching at varying levels to assist individual learners with understanding a topic area or concept (as per their needs and academic performance). In the local college the lesson plans used to have sections on differentiation activities, and learning outcomes set as "All students should be able to ...", "Some students will know ...". Students who completed the first task could then move onto doing the more difficult worksheet, or additional tasks for the higher-level work (tiered tasks). This used to result in some students doing all the tasks, and other students just doing the tasks that were compulsory.

Adaptive teaching (a contemporary approach) on the other hand is about setting high standards for the entire cohort being taught, and then making custom-made teaching strategies to support students as per the level they are at, in order for the whole class to achieve the same high standard set for all (Wharton, 2023). These are some of the hallmarks of adaptive teaching, which diverge from differentiation. By assessing student demographics within a class and looking at different ethnicities, additional learning needs and whether or not English is their first language, this helps teachers to engineer customised learning resources to germinate enhancements in teaching delivery (improving academic student success rates). It evidences working towards standard 5 of the DFE Teachers' Standards (DFE, 2024). Afterwards all students can then use the newly acquired skills and learning to help them advance in different ways (some examples are shared below):

Student Success Stories from the Application of Contemporary Approaches in STEM teaching

Example 1
By placing a strong emphasis on researcher skills development for all students on the higher education course, it comprised in one student having their research project being published in a journal for mental health. Aiding wider skills growth in students is essential for their future STEM practice.

Example 2

A second student has used their newly improved academic writing skills, and clinical knowledge acquired on the course as an alternative entry route to higher education. This student is now in her second year studying a Master's in Public Health, following completion of a self-directed higher education course. Again, wider skills advancement is critical in maximising opportunities for all learners, regardless of the age they are at.

Example 3

Another now works at Band 6 level as a Specialist Anticoagulation pharmacy technician, providing care and monitoring for patients in their practice prescribed anticoagulation drugs in an NHS setting. Anticoagulant drugs are used to prevent clots for patients at high risk of experiencing them, for instance if they have serious cardiovascular conditions such as atrial fibrillation. These drugs reduce their risk of experiencing heart attacks, strokes, or venous thromboembolic events such as pulmonary embolism or deep vein thrombosis. Patients on these anticoagulant drugs require close patient monitoring (NHS, 2021).

Considering that students on healthcare, and STEM courses are predicated in critical areas as the example demonstrates, these areas are subject to continual updates in practice. Within the last decade in the UK there have been four new anticoagulant drugs that have been approved by National Institute for Health and Care Excellence (NICE) to be prescribed in these situations. These drugs can cause side effects such as bleeding and require dose adjustments for patients with renal impairment. Patient renal function (kidney function) needs to be closely monitored. They can interact with other drugs heightening the risk of bleeds.

Case study-based learning was used to contextualise learning resources to foster deeper learning for all students. The case studies devised by the lecturer reflected the most current guidelines for treatments, which exemplifies the significance of STEM teachers/lecturers keeping up to date with CPD (continuing professional development). They were related to patient monitoring required for these drugs and encouraged problem-solving skills to be sharpened by setting the clinical content in the real world (Mind Tools Ltd, 2024). In turn it inspired the learner to complete a research project for the course to improve safer prescribing and ensure up-to-date regular patient monitoring with these newer anticoagulant drugs. Some elements of the local research project had similarities with an approach to research that is action research based. An issue was identified, and interventions used to overcome the issue were assessed simultaneously whilst they were being implemented. It was the student local research project from the course that impressed their workplace managers and led to the student being promoted at work.

Adaptive teaching and case study-based learning are particularly prominent in own teaching practice. Learning theories like these can be employed in helping to design interventions to support a particular area requiring intervention and can be incredibly valuable in action research projects.

To sum up teachers have many roles and responsibilities and encouraging more local/action research (albeit appropriately funded) could assist teachers old and new to the profession to exercise more input to address contemporary issues discussed. Fittingly, this may permit new pathways for career progression, and networking opportunities to improve regional inequalities in education attainment levels. Employing action research in this manner is underpinned in principle 12 (see Appendix 6) for the Global Framework of Professional Teaching Standards (Education International and UNESCO, 2022).

Again, the appropriate use of AI can be beneficial to teaching and STEM disciplines, but safeguards must be in place to ensure information acquired in this manner is substantiated. Having quality assurance mechanisms interwoven with local research and ensuring safe conduct in research for different parties is key in augmenting areas with flaws. Lecturers encouraging strong researcher skills development for their students can lead to positive outcomes for the students and improve their future STEM practice.

A free quiz can be accessed by readers of the book to test their knowledge on this chapter, by using a Smartphone to scan the following QR code or the readers can click the link below:

<https://forms.office.com/e/3Bms4Rkmeu?origin=lprLink>

Bibliography

Department for Education. (2024) *Initial Teacher Training and Early Career Framework.* [Online] Available from: <https://www.gov.uk/government/publications/initial-teacher-training-and-early-career-framework>. [Accessed 24 August 2024].

Education International and UNESCO. (2022) *Global Framework of Professional Teaching Standards.* [Online] Available from: <https://www.ei-ie.org/en/item/25734:global-framework-of-professional-teaching-standards.> [Accessed 01 July 2023].

Gravells, A. (2014). *The Award in Education and Training.* London: SAGE.

Guardian News & Media Limited. (2022) *44% of Teachers in England Plan to Quit within Five Years.* <https://www.theguardian.com/education/2022/apr/11/teachers-england-plan-to-quit-workloads-stress-trust#:~:text=Ahead%20of%20the%20National%20Education,would%20leave%20within%20two%20years.>. [Accessed 26 August 2024].

Holtrop, S. D. (1997) Christian Philosophy of Education: A Responsibility Model. In H. Van Brummelen & D. C. Elliott (Eds.), *Nurturing Christians as Reflective Educators.* Claremont, CA: Learning Light.

Milmo and Agency. (2023) *Two US Lawyers Fined for Submitting Fake Court Citations from ChatGPT.* [Online] Available from: <https://www.theguardian.com/technology/2023/jun/23/two-us-lawyers-fined-submitting-fake-court-citations-chatgpt>. [Accessed 24 June 2023].

MIND. (2023) *Facts and Figures about Young People and Mental Health*. [Online] Available from: <https://www.mind.org.uk/about-us/our-strategy/doing-more-for-young-people/facts-and-figures-about-young-people-and-mental-health/>. [Accessed 08 June 2023].

Mind Tools Ltd. (2024) *Case Study-Based Learning Enhancing Learning Through Immediate Application*. [Online] Available from: <https://www.mindtools.com/ar8cfge/case-study-based-learning>. [Accessed 08 March 2024].

NHS. (2021) *Overview Anticoagulant Medicines*. [Online] Available from: <https://www.nhs.uk/conditions/anticoagulants/>. [Accessed 06 November 2023].

Wharton, J. (2023) *How to get Adaptive Teaching Right*. [Online] Available from: How teachers can make the most of adaptive teaching | Tes. [Accessed 07 June 2023].

CHAPTER 2

Tips for Academic and Reflective Writing

Introduction

In Chapter 2, the key differences between academic and reflective writing will be conveyed. In addition, tips will be supplied on formatting too with a full reflective account to demonstrate the layout for reflective writing. This reflective account was published in the Impact Journal for the Chartered College of Teaching in 2021.

The action research project report presented in Chapter 7 on the other hand exemplifies the format of report writing and exhibits the writing style used in academically written pieces. Sometimes teaching on courses in particular STEM courses may not devote enough attention in optimising general academic and reflective writing principles, hence student assignments may exhibit weaknesses in these facets that then continues on in their STEM practice.

The example action research project report in Chapter 7 will assist researchers at varying levels in different areas to appreciate the importance of maintaining objectivity within research, and in preserving academic integrity. It will be a strong example for teachers and educators carrying out local/action research and serves as a guide to set out the structure of a local research report in practice.

With reflective writing such as reflective accounts or reflective diaries it is aired in an evaluative manner using the first-person narrative differing fundamentally to academic writing. Think about it as writing about your reflective thinking in conjunction with your teaching/practice and capturing the implications of theory. Academic writing though is objective and is written in the third-person narrative. Both use formal language and have a formal structure!

Reflective Practice in Teaching

Reflection is fundamental to evolving teaching pedagogy (method and practice of teaching). Superficial reflections may mean a loss of opportunity for professional development. Completing an all-embracing reflection allows for deeper levels of insight to be collated on the good aspects of teaching practice and uncover the areas which require further refinement. Due to the vast array of duties, and responsibilities placed on teachers and educators completing a rich reflection to accomplish this is not always achievable. Most researchers in the field would unyieldingly argue for periodic reflections to be undertaken on teaching practice.

Upon self-reflection I would argue that I alongside other teaching staff must face this frequently, where time and conflicts between managerial demands, pastoral care and teaching means less time is afforded to deep introspection. One personal example from own teaching practice, which springs to mind that exemplifies a common problem is the collapsing of timetables for teaching slots recently on short notice. This meant very little time was awarded to reflection due to other overriding commitments to update the lesson resources and learning strategies in an even more reduced space of time than originally anticipated (Randle and Brady, 2007). The shortage of teaching staff in the vocational sciences department compounded this issue and echoes the ongoing national shortage of STEM teachers.

At different points of the teacher training journey many may muse on why they should complete regular reflections, but the reflections can produce improvements in teaching practice. It keeps lecturers/teachers motivated to keep innovating, and to take on board all they can with the new learning theories they are coming across to enlighten their own teaching pedagogy. Lecturers are able to assess where they are with their current practice and acknowledge any shortcomings in their teaching. Teachers need to be thick-skinned with a capacity to take on board constructive critique, and advice from their peers, their students, and other stakeholders. Another key element which should be contemplated is that teaching staff may not be able to solve everything on their own for the critical issue identified. Effective change needs consultation with others and collaborating with team members to advance teaching delivery for all. It is essential therefore to undertake a detailed examination on what teachers do well when teaching, share good practice, and it is equally valuable to contemplate reflexivity on where teachers can progress as individuals and as a team. From a STEM practice perspective reflection can help unearth blind spots in practice in different STEM fields and inform future CPD opportunities.

Reflecting on STEM Updates in Practice

Wider contemporary issues facing pharmacy and healthcare are reviewed in this section to establish the importance of reflection in directing future CPD, but this is just as important in many other STEM disciplines. Pharmacy and healthcare are based in continuously changing landscapes. It is vital to keep abreast of changes in microbiology through independent CPD, such as on new advances emerging on phage therapy covered in recent times in a BBC report on their potential in combatting the global threat of antibiotic resistance (Gallagher, 2019). This is a major example of how bigger critical issues facing STEM teachers (especially for healthcare courses) needs to be surveyed against changing guidance in the field. It evidences working in line with standard 8 of the Professional standards for teachers and trainers (ETF, 2022), and the joint EI/UNESCO standard 10 of the Professional Teaching Standards (Education International and UNESCO, 2022). See appendices 5 and 6. It shines a light on why teaching should not be separate to practice, and to factor in new updates in practice to ensure learning materials reflect the most recent updates.

Taking the contemporary issue of antibiotic resistance levels on the rise. This, coupled with not many new antibiotics being licensed, could mean that antibiotics are ineffective for treating infections resulting in greater numbers of fatalities for future generations. There is ongoing research in this area. Bacteriophages (or phages) are a type of virus, which are used to treat bacterial infections. For students on healthcare courses, it is necessary to instil antimicrobial stewardship to ensure sagacious use of antibiotics and help reduce antibiotic resistance. This is just one STEM example from a pharmacy/healthcare perspective, which stresses the need for lecturers to contemplate broader STEM issues facing contemporary practice.

Recent publications by the World Health Organisation (WHO) compiled a list of priority fungal pathogens. Surveillance data is demonstrating increasing levels of antifungal resistance. Even though fungi reproduce slower than bacteria or viruses, the lack of research into new antifungal pharmacological agents is another concern as antifungal resistance levels are on the rise too (WHO, 2022). CPD conducted on these areas allowed the lecturer to update the course materials to reflect on these wider contemporary STEM issues facing their field. This helps ensure learning materials reflect the most current trends and guidelines.

Reflection is essential to course enhancement, and propelling movements forward. The exemplar published teacher reflective account included overleaf supplies a blueprint on organising reflective accounts. It disseminates the advantages and disadvantages of the main reflective models (this is not a comprehensive list, and there are many other reflective models out there):

A Reflection on Course Updates and Quality Assurance for a Newly Qualified Teacher during the Pandemic

- Teacher Reflection

Written by: Saba Ahmed

- Published on: 12 September 2021

Tips for Academic and Reflective Writing

Figure 3. Impact Journal Image on Lenses (Unknown, 2021)
8-minute read

Saba Ahmed, Pharmacy Course Revisions Lead at Bradford College and Associate Lecturer at Arden University

Introduction

During August 2020, I was tasked with updating course materials for the "Respiratory disorders" lesson on the higher education (HE) BTEC Level 4 Professional Diploma in Pharmacy Clinical Services course that I teach on at my local FE (further education) college situated in West Yorkshire. I am a dual professional, now mainly teaching HE science disciplines and occasionally undertaking locum work as a registered pharmacist to keep a hand in practice. Recently I completed the Level

7 Postgraduate Diploma in Education and Training, and I have started my second year in my teaching post. The course I teach on is for registered pharmacy technicians. It is a self-directed CPD course, delivered remotely, and it supports learners with clinical knowledge development as well as enhancing clinical skills. Courses such as these are crucial to support registered pharmacy professionals in maintaining their CPD and are critical to revalidation. I will be using the Brookfield's critical lenses model of reflection (2017) to complete this reflection, to showcase how integral each lens is in the quality assurance aspect of course updates for HE healthcare courses, when supporting NHS pharmacy teams in different settings. The four lenses are:

- own perspective (scrutinising this through the autobiographical lens by considering the previous experiences of the individual, their thoughts, and feelings)
- theoretical perspective (assessing the incident to determine if relevant guidelines, policies, and published research can provide further insight)
- peer lens (taking into consideration the advice and experience of more senior colleagues and other professionals)
- student vantage point (giving the student voice an adequate platform and understanding it from a learner experience).

As Gibbs (1988, cited in the University of Birmingham, 2015) puts it:

> It is not sufficient to have an experience to learn. Without reflecting on this experience, it may be quickly forgotten, or its learning potential lost. (p. 9)

Throughout my practice so far, I have found using Brookfield's critical lenses (2017) over other reflective models such as the Gibbs Reflective Cycle (1988) more impactful to teaching undertaken on healthcare courses. Even though, post-registration many healthcare professionals may use the latter model, where it can serve as a reflective exercise to learn from a critical incident such as a medication error. Yet it does not delve deep enough to factor in the student perspective for trainee/newly registered healthcare professionals undertaking HE courses, and does not accommodate wider contexts such as current guidelines and theoretical knowledge related to the area of practice in a concrete manner (University of Birmingham, 2015). The same can be expressed for other models that I have come across, such as Rolfe et al.'s "What?

So what? Now what?" reflective model (2001, cited in University of Connecticut, n.d.).

This model again asks key questions to help learn from a serious incident to understand the nature of the event/incident (What?), the impact of the said event/incident (So what?) and finally next steps required (Now what?), which are fundamental elements to ongoing CPD for healthcare professionals in practice and those undertaking courses to facilitate expansion of clinical knowledge. Nevertheless, it does not accomplish this in a detailed enough manner, where deep introspection should be undertaken using a multifaceted approach to enable learners to deliberate on how an incident could aid in identifying future CPD opportunities. Additionally, the other models don't consider how incidents coincide with local or national guidelines, whereas the theoretical perspective of Brookfield's reflective model (1995) challenges learners and teachers to assess issues from the vantage point of literature and guidelines published in the area. Other models in my opinion don't go far enough to challenge individual healthcare professionals and lecturers teaching a science discipline to assess how their practice may have gaps in local protocols and national NHS agendas. Examining this in a broad sense, I would argue that the other models of reflection may be somewhat effective in gaining an insight into how course updates or assessments can be improved upon. There is a deficit nonetheless, in appreciating how changes in practice and updates in theoretical knowledge for all disciplines should impact on quality assurance in course updates or day-to-day teaching.

Applying Brookfield's Model of Reflection (1995)

The remainder of this reflective account will focus on how a rich reflection using the four critical lenses of Brookfield's model (1995) was used as a quality assurance mechanism to improve course materials for the course on which I teach.

Reviewing this through the autobiographical and theoretical lenses, I realised that this course needed revising, as newer drugs in respiratory disorders had recently been licenced and the lesson needed to incorporate these to ensure that the students had up-to-date knowledge on the current treatments available.

Analysing this through the theoretical lens as a newly qualified lecturer, I ruminated on learning theories that I had learnt about as part of my studies for the level 7 PG diploma in Education and Training mainly focusing on how constructivism, humanism and situated learning theory are quite central to my teaching practice. Updating course materials to reflect the current pandemic and how pharmacy professionals can help to dispel myths was something I wanted to concentrate on therefore. By making learning more connected to current events, the learning becomes much more tangible and relevant for students on any course. As an unintentional consequence, the pandemic has offered this opportunity for all disciplines to revise learning materials.

Bearing this in mind, I constructed a case study for the online learning materials for the formative assessments, with questions set to portray how vital pharmacy professionals can be in educating patients and in tackling misleading social media posts. Such tasks, centring on situated learning theory blended with constructivism elements, help gain an improvement in clinical research skills and assist learners to reflect on what happens at the grassroots level in clinical settings to generate advances in clinical pharmacy service provision. By amalgamating different learning theories with clinical content from my own pharmacy practice, especially that stemming from my work at NHS 111 it helped me to formulate learning activities that enable significant learning to take place for the students in an authentic context. It informed how humanism and constructivist theories and aspects of situated learning theory could assist in the course renovations that I was completing (Scales, 2008). Although this was probably something felt by all with the many difficulties associated with online teaching, I felt that time was in short supply for this aspect of my teaching.

I used the second case study in this course to emphasise the dangers of shisha use, and its links to increasing the risk of acquiring serious medical conditions such as respiratory diseases and cardiac medical disorders (British Heart Foundation, n.d.). From my practice in my second role as a pharmacist, I have noted that this can often be overlooked and is worthwhile exploring and educating patients on, especially in respect of younger patients. Such consultations should foster patients to be partners in the decisions made in improving their health, and rather than just delivering patient education; an enabling approach to taking charge of their own health should be implemented. Having a patient focus allows the patient to convey any impediments to realising health goals, and a non-judgemental style in consultations can improve adherence to adopting a healthier behaviour.

Assessing the original course from the student perspective I found from previous student evaluations that one website link was no longer functioning, and some of the students had remarked that they "would have preferred some visual resources to break the text in the lesson". A sentiment shared from the peer perspective where the course lead agreed with this comment. Using Brookfield's lenses, this facilitated a rich reflection from different perspectives including the student voice being given a suitable platform. It served as a quality assurance measure to help me to revise the course (Brookfield, 2017). Armed with this knowledge, I then sourced reputable videos on asthma pathophysiology online to help make the lesson more visually stimulating. This supports learners who prefer more visual stimuli and is supported by researchers such as Roell (2019).

I garnered more from the peer perspective by sharing the first draft of the newly updated course materials with my fellow course lecturers. It added another layer for effective checks in the quality assurance process for course updates at our local college. I was able to gather valuable feedback to help me edit the lessons such as removing another website link that no longer worked, and to help restructure the pharmacological treatments used in respiratory diseases in a more succinct fashion within the online lesson materials.

Collaborative practice like this between peers helps to forge a strong sense of community of practice, which is important to foster to reduce the isolation felt from lone working as a lecturer (Kennedy, 2005), as experienced in August last year, when the guidance from my local FE establishment recommended teaching staff to continue working remotely where possible. The government guidance on COVID-19 restrictions last year was ever-changing, and locally there were variations. In the area in which

I am based, the local guidance was more attuned with the high local infection rates at the time.

Pre-COVID-19, my community of practice was based at the college, where I was able to seek advice on teaching and on course materials within the staffroom during breaks. Yet during the lockdown period such readily available access to more experienced lecturers was difficult to obtain. Guidance for FE settings during the pandemic was not static, with my FE setting considering the high infection rates and thus the advice was to encourage all teaching staff to work remotely where possible. Our teaching team had to contend with challenges such as remote working and teaching using online platforms (with the bustling nature of busy homes including cameos on online lessons from children and pets, and sometimes intermittent internet connections; just a few of the obstacles that we all most likely experienced). We therefore had to operate technology to better effect to form a digital community of practice, where the hub of lecturers used Microsoft Teams and internal emailing systems alongside WhatsApp and Telegram to keep in touch and help on any issues. This provided much-needed support, especially for those new to the profession such as myself. I was able to share my course updates with more experienced teaching staff, so they could provide advice on where to make further enhancements.

Conclusion

Conducting a thorough analysis using different lenses was of paramount importance to help ensure that I effectively updated the course materials. This is my second year of teaching actively, and scrutinising the lesson in this level of detail under different angles was indescribably valuable for the course updates aspect of my teaching practice. I hope that the newly revamped lessons are well received by all, and the new academic year will shed light on this and on any possible further tweaks required. Quality assurance measures should not be dismissed as a tick-box exercise. In my opinion they are essential to achieving quality improvement in education and in ensuring that courses remain current to reflect changes in practice, which is necessary for all courses.

Reflective Writing

The published reflective account sets the depth required for reflections and personifies the importance of reflective practice in teaching. As can be observed the writing style diverges from academic writing. In reflective pieces a more personal tone is taken, although theory should still be embraced in a substantial manner. Reflective accounts can help you zone in on metacognition elements and link it to enhancing your teaching practice or STEM practice. In many STEM professions including for pharmacy CPD reflective accounts, and reflective practice may be necessary for revalidation for future STEM professionals (GPhC, 2023).

Educational theory should still be duly deliberated on in reflective accounts in partnership with an examination of the impact of learning theories on issues, and aspects of good practice highlighted in teaching delivery to then formulate next steps. It is of the utmost importance to continually maintain the connectivity with personal action plans, and that the action plan could be redirected with each reflection.

For each reflective account provide the backdrop for each observation, and frame external pressures and internal feelings that affected the teaching delivery. Choose the reflective models which serve best to assess how the experience, and learning from it can translate into practice. Some of the reflective models offer better templates to achieve these over others, and reflective models include the Brookfield's Critical Lenses (1995), Gibbs' Reflective Cycle (1988), the DIEP model of reflection (1985), Rolfe's Reflective Model (2001), and the Atkins and Murphy Cyclical Model (1993). This list is not exhaustive, and there are other reflective models out there.

The Merits of Developing the Reflective Practitioner

Many STEM disciplines champion reflective practice to learn from a mistake or a near miss. In these reflections analyse the situation from the autobiographical lens, wider theory and guidelines, service user perspective and peer lens. A deep reflection like this could help devise a concrete set of action points to reduce the risk of the near miss or mistakes from recurring and support effective governance measures to improve services in STEM disciplines. Learning can be shared, and weaknesses could be flipped to present areas of opportunities to uplift practice.

In Appendix 3, there is another reflective account shared from own STEM teaching practice to make evident the boons of reflection in achieving genuine improvements in teaching. Appendix 3 shows how reflection can support in career advancement and was the reflective account for a fellow of the higher education academy (FHEA) application which was successful. It was a summary of my reflective practice in teaching, and again underpins the importance of using quality assurance and holistic reflections to renovate course materials. Course renovations should not be viewed as a tick-box exercise. Reflective practice could assist in directing own career progression and goal setting as well.

Academic Writing

Academic writing on the other hand has a more formal approach and has a strong orientation in evidence-based research. The academic writing style is more impartial and detached, whereas reflective writing is more personal and uses "I" more so. In academic writing "I" would not be apt to use. For both styles of writing, it is essential that points are clearly established, and refrain from using language where the aspect being relayed across is not presented as an absolute truth unless this can be 100 per cent evidenced in reputable supportive literature.

Essays and Reports

Examples of academic writing include essays and reports. Reports are more common in STEM disciplines, therefore as described previously refining analytical research skills to validate points articulated and literacy skills advancement are chief for STEM learners in their future practice. It may be commonplace for STEM professionals to compile reports for their organisation. The example action research project report in Chapter 7 exemplifies key principles of research, report writing, and how to structure reports in general. Again, this reinforces the point of not observing teaching in a vacuum. It is important to view teaching on STEM courses in the broader context. Teaching is important in raising researcher skills, and problem-solving capabilities to prepare students for their future STEM careers. The example report in Chapter 7 depicts how objectivity was maintained within academic writing and frames the clear use of evidence-based practice in action research projects.

Reports are much more concise with formal structures and are usually used to dissect results and findings. In comparison to essays, reports will most likely have shorter paragraphs, but the work should be appropriately referenced throughout to uphold academic credibility. In contrast an essay will most likely have longer paragraphs. Essays are used to probe the learners' thoughts strengthened with sufficient evidence (reputable sources) on a particular topic presented to their lecturer or academic tutor. Again, in an academically credible manner (University of Leeds, 2023).

As stated previously the writing style and language used in your report will vary in accordance with the type of report being conducted and target audience. The following subheadings are used to chunk a report:

- Title Page
- Abstract (or Executive Summary if it's a business report)
- Contents page
- Introduction/Rationale/Background with clear aims and objectives
- Literature review if it is a research project report
- Methodology
- Results
- Results/Findings Discussion
- Conclusion/Further Recommendations
- References
- Appendices

Hopefully these distinctions clarify the components in reflective writing, and academic writing. The chapter evidences the benefits of a developed reflective practitioner. A wise tip for anyone doing an assignment is to start with a blank Microsoft Word document and put some subheadings to structure the work (the start of a skeleton for your written assignment). Methodically work through the learning outcomes that need to be evidenced systematically. This helps break down the research for the assignment. Write accordingly as per the assignment brief (either academically written if it is an essay or report or write in a reflective manner if it is a reflective account). During the editing stage remove the subheadings if this works better and maintain cohesion in the work by using words which connect paragraphs. This in turn maintains the common threads in the written work.

The main differences between essay writing and report writing have been summarised. To sum up academic writing is much more objective and impersonal language is used, whereas in reflective writing the writing style can be more personal and reflective models are worthwhile to use. In both academic and reflective writing, the written work uses formal language (not colloquialisms or slang). They have formal structures, and related theory needs to be examined. A third example (from own practice) of a reflective account can be accessed by visiting the web page below from the author website:

<https://stemlecturerjourney.wordpress.com/observations/>.

A free quiz can be accessed by readers of the book to test their knowledge on this chapter, by using a Smartphone to scan the following QR code or the readers can click the link below:

<https://forms.office.com/e/xKBguxPven?origin=lprLink>

Bibliography

Ahmed, S. (2021) A Reflection on Course Updates and Quality Assurance for a Newly Qualified Teacher during the Pandemic. *Impact*, [Online] (13), [no pagination]. Available from: <https://my.chartered.college/impact_article/a-reflection-on-course-updates-and-quality-assurance-for-a-newly-qualified-teacher-during-the-pandemic/>. [Accessed 18 February 2024].

British Heart Foundation. (n.d.) *Shisha*. [Online] Available from: <www.bhf.org.uk/informationsupport/risk-factors/smoking/shisha>. [Accessed 4 July 2021].

Brookfield, S. D. (1995) *Becoming a Critically Reflective Teacher*. San Francisco: Jossey-Bass.

Brookfield, S. D. (2017) *Becoming a Critically Reflective Teacher*. 2nd edn. San Francisco: Jossey-Bass.

Education and Training Foundation. (2022) *Professional Standards*. [Online] Available from: <https://www.et-foundation.co.uk/professional-standards/>. [Accessed 24 September 2022].

Education International and UNESCO. (2022) *Global Framework of Professional Teaching Standards*. [Online] Available from: <https://www.ei-ie.org/en/item/25734:global-framework-of-professional-teaching-standards>. [Accessed 24 August 2024].

Gallagher, J. (2019) *Phage Therapy: "Viral cocktail saved my daughter's life"*. [Online] Available from: <https://www.bbc.co.uk/news/health-48199915>. [Accessed on 09 October 2022].

GPhC. (2023) *Revalidation for Pharmacists and Pharmacy Technicians*. [Online] Available from: <https://www.pharmacyregulation.org/revalidation>. [Accessed 24 June 2023].

Kennedy, A. (2005) Models of Continuing Professional Development: A Framework for Analysis. *Journals of In-service Education*, 31(2), pp. 235–250.

Randle, K., and Brady, N. (2007) Further Education and the New Managerialism. *Journal of Further and Higher Education*, 21(2), pp. 229–239.

Roell, K. (2019) *The Visual Learning Style*. [Online] Available from: <https://www.thoughtco.com/visual-learning-style-3212062>. [Accessed 26 August 2024].

Scales, P. (2008) *Teaching in the Lifelong Learning Sector*. Maidenhead: Open University Press.

UCONN. (2001) *What? So What? Now What? Model*. [Online] Available from: <https://edtech.uconn.edu/multimedia-consultation__trashed/portfolios/reflection-models/>. [Accessed 24 August 2024].

University of Birmingham. (2015) *A Short Guide to Reflective Writing.* [Online] Available from: <https://intranet.birmingham.ac.uk/as/libraryservices/library/asc/documents/public/Short-Guide-Reflective-Writing.pdf.> [Accessed 03 July 2022].

University of Connecticut. (n.d.) *Reflection Models.* [Online] Available from: <https://edtech.uconn.edu/multimedia-consultation/portfolios/reflection-models/#>. [Accessed 03 July 2022].

University of Leeds. (2023) *Report Writing.* [Online] Available from: <https://library.leeds.ac.uk/info/14011/writing/114/report_writing>. [Accessed 24 June 2023].

WHO. (2022) *WHO Fungal Priority Pathogens List to Guide Research, Development and Public Health Action.* [Online] Available from: <https://www.who.int/publications/i/item/9789240060241>. [Accessed 12 March 2023].

CHAPTER 3

Demystifying Basic Research Terminology

Introduction

The main goal for this chapter is to serve as a reminder of key research terminology, or it may help those who are conducting their first-ever research project. A refresher on specialist research terminology can hopefully untangle them and lend aid in supporting researcher skills development. Having a firm command of these different terms for teaching staff can elevate teaching on courses with research projects or dissertation modules, in turn better equipping students with critical analysis skills for their future careers.

To start off with the key differences between the three main types of research methodologies quantitative/qualitative/mixed research methodologies will be outlined.

Research Methodology Types

A research methodology is the mode of research used in an investigation/action research project to gather results on a research topic in a reliable way. Whether the research methodology is quantitative/qualitative or a combination of the two (known as a mixed research methodology) is largely dependent on the topic area being researched, and resources available. Quantitative research methodologies are associated with numerical data and analysis of statistics, whereas a qualitative research methodology is linked to non-numerical data. Sometimes a mixed research methodology is used in research projects, which is the research methodology chronicled in the action research project shared in Chapter 7.

The research methodology selected, and data collation methods chosen should be backed by solid justification. Clear steps need to be set out on how the research methodology will be implemented (NICE, 2022). It should be relevant to the topic/research area, and sync with the aims and objectives of the research project. An aim/ aims establish the overall intent, strategic direction, and purpose of the research project. Objectives break down the aims into specific targets, to enable the delivery and execution of the research project aims. Practical considerations and ethics need to be mulled over, to provide reasoning as to why one research methodology was more appropriate over others.

Extending quantitative and qualitative research further with quantitative research it is more concerned with numerical data and being able to quantify and generalise outcomes and results of the research project. One set of facts is studied in relation to another set of facts. On the other hand, qualitative data in research is more closely connected to individual opinions and less associated with statistical analysis. If the data cannot be counted it is qualitative, and a richer exploration of data captured could be uncovered (NICE, 2022).

Sometimes a mixture of quantitative and qualitative data acquisition is used, and the method or methods selected must be complementary to the subject being researched. Case studies (a qualitative approach) may be needed, when assessing the impact of a medical intervention on the quality of life for patients in a study. A quantitative approach (possibly through questionnaires) to identify the likelihood of side effects from medicines granted recent marketing authorisations, could be more suitable in gathering post-marketing surveillance data. The latter would require examination of statistics acquired and would be conducted on a larger scale. The case studies would be completed on a smaller scale. Nonetheless the case study-based research could facilitate a deeper dissemination of findings (that being said on a much micro scale though).

To further contextualise in an educational setting a quantitative approach may be used in assessing differences in grade attainment after a particular intervention is set, and then compared against datasets from previous years. The research project may evolve, and a qualitative approach may be justified to gain opinions on the intervention from the student perspective. To acquire the student perspective, a student forum could be held to gain more in-depth qualitative data. Other research terms that researchers will come across commonly include primary and secondary data.

Primary and Secondary Data

Primary data is acquiring data first hand through different methods such as observational studies, student questionnaires or interviews etc. Secondary data is reviewing published data such as a systematic review, or meta-analysis. In action research projects it is likely to involve primary data acquisition, such as on gathering data related to student attainment levels to appraise the success of an intervention. Action research is about simultaneously conducting research and applying an action or actions to resolve an identified issue in teaching. In the introduction action research is relayed across in much deeper detail.

Yet in the literature review for the action research project, this would have secondary data from published research to inform the research design and rationale for the project. Being able to appreciate research terminology and dissect the types of published data to inform rationales in action research projects/local research is paramount to guiding advances in STEM practice and in educational research. Local research/action research needs to be underscored by a strong foundation to validate potential interventions chosen.

Meta-Analysis

A meta-analysis (a form of secondary research) combines the outcomes of multiple studies to draw conclusions and support opinions to explain findings or variations (think of it as a mega analysis on many studies). It could answer a question more broadly than any individual study, such as on the effects of COVID-19 on several populations? Historically meta-analysis research was first used in education, but now would be utilised more in the fields of medicine and psychology. If used in educational research, it can serve as a pooled analysis of previously published action research studies, or other studies to harvest a more precise estimate in comparison to any individual research study. They may settle disparities in studies that have conflicting results, and outcomes to explain variations observed in said conflicting studies (Durham University, 2017).

Systematic Review

Another type of secondary research that readers may come across is a systematic review, which is where a specific statistical strategy is employed as per the research topic under investigation. The systematic approach in the methods used in the systematic review reduces bias and contains clear inclusion and exclusion criteria. Within a systematic review data from published studies on the defined topic is reviewed, and interpreted (a guided filtration, so to speak). The published data is critically appraised and summarised interpretations are refined into an evidence-based conclusion.

A systematic review shares overlap with meta-analysis and is a means of reviewing and judging data in a systematic approach to answer a well-defined question. Systematic reviews could help inform teaching pedagogy, and future local action research projects or upcoming cycles of research projects. As a hypothetical example of a well-defined question, this could be "Are data handling processes in education settings steadfast enough to prevent data leaks"? Most would affirm that systematic reviews and meta-analysis, or better yet a systematic review combined with a meta-analysis would hold top ranking on the different types of evidence published.

Interpreting Secondary Research with a Pinch of Salt

Continuing with secondary research published, sometimes the evidence base may not be so strong, or the quality of the evidence may not be to a high standard. As an example, there are many companies that sell collagen-based products with many health claims purported to them. Claims include younger-looking skin and healthier hair. These claims are normally based on small studies. Variables such as an improved diet may not be accounted for, or the study may not have a control group.

There may not be any randomised controlled trials, systematic reviews, or a meta-analysis to back these claims. The research could be carried out by the company themselves. Would the shareholders have a vested interest? Is there independent research to substantiate claims made? These are factors that need to be assessed diligently, when examining secondary research. In addition to this protein which collagen is, when consumed by the oral route will be broken down by the stomach acid into its monomer amino acids. This will then be used to create any type of protein the body requires (enzymes, insulin, haemoglobin, possibly collagen etc.). With this in mind do the collagen supplements/drinks offer any distinct advantage over just incorporating more protein in the diet naturally? For these types of articles/published research, it is essential to weigh up the accuracy of the evidence presented to be able to make conclusions about the claims being made. Examining the rigour is imperative, for instance who/what group or organisation are affiliated with the research (are there any conflicts of interest?). Is the research peer-reviewed? It underlines the notion that the type of research being evaluated needs deep inspection, because when individuals unpick the data or examine the methodology or claims made in the research they may not seem as solid as they are advertised at first glance. This applies to all fields of research including educational research. If AI systems were used to collate data like this, again the researcher needs to apply critical analysis, and filter what has been presented to deem whether the secondary research is reliable, authentic, accurate, and credible.

Literature Review

Moving onto literature reviews (secondary research) these can be used in the teaching world to acquire the theoretical perspective under the Brookfield's lenses to support a specific novel intervention being trialled in teaching practice, or use of learning theory in teaching in action research. There are numerous types of literature reviews, of which the four main types are:

1. Narrative reviews are quite useful to examine a topic in a broad sense and could provide historical context in a joined-up manner. Potentially these could be biased though.
2. Systematic reviews (see earlier section on systematic reviews for more details). These could be quite in depth.
3. Meta-analysis (again see the previous section), these provide a firm analysis using multiple studies to draw general conclusions in a more quantifiable way. A meta-analysis could be more apt for studies that are more quantitative and have more of a statistical analysis orientation.
4. Scoping reviews could be of value in horizon scanning for issues early in the research, through reviewing published secondary information to help identify gaps and make the research question clearer. These could be of use in pilot studies too.

In any piece of research and for any type of literature review in any field including STEM areas, the evidence assessed must be examined for robustness, reliability, relevance and ensure the design of the secondary research is not flawed. For example, that researcher bias has not crept in where the results are represented in a certain light that corresponds with the researcher opinions and ambitions (CORE, 2019). Make sure the research isn't outdated as well. These are areas scrutinised using the well-known acronym CRAAP.

- Assess the currency of the information
- Analyse the relevance of the evidence to the research requirements
- Look at the authority of the information (credentials of the authors, sponsors/backers of the research and reputability of the source)
- Examine the accuracy (reliability of the research, peer reviewed or not, and the quality of the evidence source; think back on the hierarchy in the quality of evidence types introduced earlier)
- Review the purpose of the research (propaganda, or to inform). (CORE, 2019)

Another useful tip with secondary data acquisition in research projects, and in conducting a literature review is to use the new comment tab on Microsoft Word to keep a tally of resources/published evidence being used. The citations in text and reference list details can be recorded in rough using the comments tab as per that section, and then when readers of the book come to format their referencing at the final stage of the research project it is less painstakingly difficult and time intensive.

Collaborative Lesson Research

Collaborative lesson research (CLR) is derived from Japanese Lesson Study for teachers. Educators research a lesson thoroughly that requires improvement, and then create a lesson plan/design to improve teaching. This is an example of a primary research method, which is qualitative in nature. Other educators or potentially a mentor could be invited to observe the new lesson, and then a peer discussion is held after the lesson to assess the successes and opportunities for development in the lesson. Good practice can be shared in this way for positive outcomes, and the discussion may yield greater insight into further refinements required. Easily this could be used to inform action research projects in teaching such as on actions used in the research, and simultaneously CLR could be used in the quality assurance aspects of the action research project. It mirrors features within the second-person action research type set out in the introduction of the book with peer input. Potentially CLR could be used to conduct a pilot action research study, and parts of the research project report shared later in the book exemplify the potential for CLR principles to be used in action research (Collaborative Lesson Research UK, n.d.).

By sharing these key terms used in research it can assist those completing action research in teaching, and other research projects. The decision to go down the route of primary or secondary, and quantitative or qualitative research is heavily influenced by the topic being investigated in the research project, ethics linked to the proposed research and practicality to carry out the research within the workplace.

Another important aspect with research is that research projects are not set in stone, where researchers may need to display flexibility in research project management skills in light of unexpected obstacles encountered. Discuss any potential limitations with peers and project supervisors to reflect on the situation and make minor tweaks to research projects in any field as applicable. Specifically, the new ITTECF framework encourages mentor contact/meetings. For anyone undertaking a research project in their teaching capacity at any stage of their career, they could have these conversations to help overcome issues by collaborating with others (DFE, 2024). Even in STEM disciplines working with others on research projects to enlighten any adjustments in research projects to overcome limitations or roadblocks is a fantastic way to gain the peer perspective and could serve as a valuable quality assurance mechanism. Collaborate with peers effectively. Their input could provide a fresh perspective and serve as a safety net within research.

Other factors to consider are current societal issues with teaching staff shortages and pandemic pressures, which could exert stressors on your action research project. The project may need to evolve accordingly. Consider such issues with other members of the teaching team (invite them to observe lessons, where delivery could be improved). This shares some of the hallmarks of a CLR approach. Discuss concerns with the project supervisor earlier on, to synthesise solutions to counter hindrances identified in research.

Anyone conducting research in STEM disciplines should consider quality assurance, and peer input to help combat obstacles experienced in practice. This is a prudent safety layer that is worthwhile to incorporate within action research or local research projects. View action research/local research in a holistic sense with a focus on current STEM practice to enable boosts in teaching on STEM disciplines, and to reflect on wider contemporary issues.

A free quiz can be accessed by readers of the book to test their knowledge on this chapter, by using a Smartphone to scan the following QR code or the readers can click the link below:

<https://forms.office.com/e/ziLB1BZgSq?origin=lprLink>

Bibliography

CORE. (2019) *Writing: Literature Reviews for Culminating Project*. [Online] Available from: <https://azhin.org/c.php?g=457546&p=3286426.> [Accessed 08 June 2023].

Department for Education. (2024) *Initial Teacher Training and Early Career Framework*. [Online] Available from: <https://www.gov.uk/government/publications/initial-teacher-training-and-early-career-framework>. [Accessed 24 August 2024].

Durham University. (2017) *Meta-synthesis and Comparative Meta-analysis of Education Research Findings: Some Risks and Benefits*. [Online] Available from: <https://dro.dur.ac.uk/17384/#:~:text=Meta%2Danalysis%2C%20or%20quantitative%20synthesis,or%20smaller%20effects%20across%20studies>. [Accessed 20 November 2022].

NICE. (2022) *Glossary*. [Online] Available from: <https://www.nice.org.uk/glossary?letter=r>. [Accessed 19 November 2022].

CHAPTER 4

An Introduction to Data Collation Methods

Introduction

The main types of methods used in data collation will be surveyed in Chapter 4. These should coincide with the research methodology (quantitative, qualitative, or mixed) for the action research project/local research project. They need to align with the aims and objectives of the project. This part of the book will deliver a quick and useful summary of the main types of methods used to collate data. Advantages and disadvantages connected to each form of data collection will be articulated.

Primary Forms of Data Collation

Questionnaires/Surveys

Good coverage of quantitative data can be acquired using this method. They could be created electronically using digital tools such as "SurveyMonkey", or researchers can create their own questionnaires/surveys on Microsoft Forms. The questions used can be closed or open. Open questions can enable the gathering of qualitative data. Closed questions, and questions with scales can be used to acquire quantitative data.

Quantitative data generated by questionnaires can be represented with the use of infographics, which was done in the action research project included later in the book (in a rudimentary fashion). Infographics is a way of expressing key statistics, and data using graphical visual representations to transmit the main takeaway points of the research to different audiences in a simple manner. Concise and clear statistics are communicated to help make sense of the research undertaken. NHS research projects use this widely to pitch important messages to the audience. Free templates to help create infographics can be located on online tools such as "Vengage" or "Piktochart" (just remember to read the website terms and conditions to maintain confidentiality in data gathered). This is a significant ethical and legal consideration to ensure data is protected, and confidentiality is maintained.

Even though researchers can get more exposure by using questionnaires, there could be low response rates. Surveys/questionnaires could be seen as a tick-box exercise by respondents/participants. This is an important feature that researchers need to factor in when assessing whether questionnaires should be used in data collation methods in their research, and on how they can be designed to encourage better response rates (NICE, 2022).

Although the data acquired can assist statistical analysis, however a more detailed appreciation of the topic may be required than what questionnaires can offer on their own. To help remedy this a combination of surveys/questionnaires could be used with interviews. In some questionnaire responses some interesting points may be relayed across that merit further investigation to procure a deeper comprehension of the issue, therefore combining data collation methods such as surveys/questionnaires (more quantitative in nature) with interviews or forums (more qualitative) could allow more insight to be determined (a mixed research methodology). It is vital that the questions posed in surveys and questionnaires are not leading as well. A peer/work colleague could screen the questions to check for bias.

Interviews/Forums

Interviews and forums have the benefit of allowing a fuller perception of the interviewees'/forum participants' opinions on a particular area to be amassed. Interviews can be conducted one on one with open or closed questions but could be time-consuming. Forums can be used to gather rich opinions from multiple people simultaneously (NICE, 2022). A wealth of qualitative data can be obtained. Possible drawbacks could include researcher bias (unconscious or conscious) seeping in to help elicit the preferred responses from the participants to purposely back the researcher narrative, and they could be time-consuming to conduct especially if individuals go off-topic. The questions and interviews/forums could become loaded. It is essential that researcher bias is minimised throughout the research project and reflect on ways to manage this. There are many opportunities for this to influence research projects inadvertently.

Another issue which a researcher may face is that quieter participants in a forum may have their voices overpowered by those that are more confident. These potential downsides could be ameliorated using semi-structured interviews. A pre-set list of questions could again be screened by a peer to ensure that objectivity is upheld, and the semi-structured approach allows flexibility in the questioning as opposed to structured interview layouts that are rigid. This is another reason, which cements the importance of peer collaboration in research projects. The questioning technique can be adapted to return the discussion to the topic being researched. Also, to encourage contributions from less forthcoming members of the forum the researcher could have a facilitative approach to encourage participation from the less vocal participants. Such approaches could be utilised in action research/local research in teaching, or in grassroots research in STEM fields depending on the topic area under investigation.

Gaining Valid Consent

For anyone taking part in a research project (participants in interviews/forums/completing questionnaires etc.), it is important to gain consent as per organisational and legal frameworks. This is another reason to ensure a good working relationship with the research project supervisor and other team members. They can provide key support, and signpost budding researchers to workplace resources that could help with the research project.

It is worthwhile to provide ample time for students or participants to raise any concerns or questions, that they may have about participating in the action research/local research project. Remember valid consent must be obtained and know the research project inside and out; this means the researcher can answer any questions that participants may pose and put them at ease.

A thorough examination of published data in the field through conducting a literature review can help researchers become expert on the topic being investigated (although apply CRAAP principles on the type of literature review conducted). Alongside this have a copy available of the confidentiality/data protection policies of the organisation, as the students/participants in the research may wish to review them before providing consent. Those participants who are unwilling to take part in the research must have their decision respected (Bell, 2005).

If information is being accessed on computer records such as on grade attainment, again those participants must provide valid consent as per the educational establishment guidelines. Confidentiality is paramount to maintain in any form of data collation and use electronic devices that are secure to ensure no data leaks occur in any form of research! This is both an important legal and ethical concern touched on earlier that needs to be deliberated on in the research project proposal, as there have been data leaks resulting in damaging consequences.

Randomised Controlled Trials

RCTs are observed more in the field of medicine and would be rarely used in education. RCTs allow numerical data to be analysed. They involve randomly assigning similar people to two or more groups. One group has the intervention being studied, and another group could have a different intervention or could be allocated as the placebo group depending on the type of RCT. In other words, the control group is where there is no intervention or variable being tested allowing a benchmark to be established, to draw comparisons in the results obtained to determine if an intervention applied made a significant difference over no intervention or treatment. Even though RCTs are judged as the gold standard in primary research in the field of medicine, they would not be used commonly in educational research. Potentially taking this approach could contravene standard 1 of the DFE Teachers' Standards, and principle 3 in the joint EI/UNESCO framework (included in appendices 4 and 6 respectively) (Department for Education, 2024; Education International and UNESCO 2022). It would be unethical to have one group of children/students being assigned an intervention which could benefit their learning, and the other group of students having no such intervention (NICE, 2022). The implications to life chances, and future prospects for students raise very questionable ethics in the design of educational research that are RCT orientated.

Ethnography

An example of qualitative research is ethnography. These are observational studies, where the researcher inserts themselves within the group, or community to observe interactions and behaviours. The researcher then draws conclusions (Bell, 2005). Teachers may do this on autopilot when they are teaching a new cohort to see which students participate more in class, and to determine the class dynamics between students. Perhaps all educators whilst in their teaching capacity do this in some shape or form in an informal manner. The challenge is formalising this to potentially make the observational research feed into augmenting learner attainment for all students as per their needs!

Experimental Research

Experimental research is mainly a type of quantitative research and is utilised in the physical sciences and other fields such as psychology or education. It is the classical scientific research platform employed in Pavlov's behaviourist well-renowned experiment with dogs being trained to salivate at the sound of a bell. The experimental technique/methodology employs making adaptations to one or more independent variable, and this change is applied to one or more dependent variable to analyse the effects on the latter. The designer of the experiment must know their subject matter being researched intricately, and randomly allocate subjects to different groups to test their hypothesis (NICE, 2022).

Secondary Data Research

Secondary data research includes reviewing anything created in the past, and potentially secondary data research could be better for the topic being investigated over primary research (it depends on the topic area). This section is more condensed as earlier chapters examine published data in more detail. Secondary resources could include government reports, local workplace reports and published data such as systematic reviews/meta-analysis or national guidelines and policies. Other examples include organisation health and safety records, press releases, published online material on websites, articles in journals and so forth (NICE, 2022). The secondary data should be assessed carefully as outlined in the literature review section in the previous chapter. There should be an appropriate secondary research methodology, which is compatible to the topic being researched. This is to ensure that the data acquired in this way is current, reliable, and valid to generate firm conclusions. The researcher should check if there are any affiliations, which may result in researcher bias influencing the secondary data results interpretation. This could make the secondary research less dependable. It should in essence meet the "craap" criteria discussed previously.

It is an accessible form of research. Most secondary data can be obtained for free (review organisation access rights) making it low cost, and extensive data could be procured. These are some of the advantages. Although one key minus is that there may not be much secondary data available on the chosen topic. In the action research project shared in Chapter 7 for the literature review there was only limited secondary data, so a narrative literature review was completed to acquire as much relevant secondary data as possible. Other downsides could be that the research is outdated or may not be wholly relevant to your research topic. Another disadvantage is that as discussed it may not be of good quality as well. After analysis of the secondary data, it may be decided that it was loaded to fit the researcher narrative, making the paper being reviewed in the research project less credible.

Reviewing secondary data can however be an indispensable form of research, and for those conducting primary research it may be incredibly useful in their literature review.

A free quiz can be accessed by readers of the book to test their knowledge on this chapter, by using a Smartphone to scan the following QR code or the readers can click the link below:

<https://forms.office.com/e/qSCJcbqpP0?origin=lprLink>

Bibliography

Bell, J. (2005) *Doing your Research Project.* 4th edn. Suffolk: Open University Press.

Department for Education. (2024) *Initial Teacher Training and Early Career Framework.* [Online] Available from: <https://www.gov.uk/government/publications/initial-teacher-training-and-early-career-framework>. [Accessed 26 August 2024].

Education International and UNESCO. (2022) *Global Framework of Professional Teaching Standards.* [Online] Available from: <https://www.ei-ie.org/en/item/25734:global-framework-of-professional-teaching-standards>. [Accessed 01 July 2023].

NICE. (2022) *Glossary.* [Online] Available from: <https://www.nice.org.uk/glossary?letter=r>. [Accessed 19 November 2022].

CHAPTER 5

Maintaining Quality Assurance

Introduction

Chapter 5 is dedicated to quality assurance in research, and in upgrading course materials. Implanting quality assurance mechanisms in research projects is necessary in safeguarding the integrity of the research, and to prevent research being purposely driven to fit the desired outcomes. At every point of the action research project/local STEM research project, bias needs to be protected against. Periodic reflections, and peer reviews employed as quality assurance measures in research projects can be powerful tools to help screen for issues that may occur in research. They can even assist in coming up with solutions to problems encountered.

The action research project proposal in the next chapter highlights the importance of quality assurance and working with peers in research projects to help overcome issues such as inadvertently making a research project too ambitious. Minor fine tuning and adjustments in response to unexpected, or expected obstacles is a critical research project management skill to hone. Such issues should be thoughtfully addressed at the proposal stage wherever possible, or as soon as the problem is identified. Letting it persist without remediation could adversely impact the final outcomes. Most research projects face hiccups along the way, but the researcher should not become deflated by them. It could end up being positive to the evolution of the research project, and lead to a deeper critical analysis. Or if it becomes unfeasible to continue with the research project due to a major flaw being discovered, then it is better to reflect and act on this in the early stages to come up with a new research project proposal that is realistic to complete.

In many research projects including action research projects or local research projects the pandemic pressures, and multiple lockdowns made it difficult to capture face-to-face data. Arrangements needed to be made to do interviews online via Microsoft Teams, or to email out questionnaires. Timelines in proposals for action research projects/local STEM research projects needed to be shifted, because it led to delays in carrying out certain parts of research projects. Reflection and collaboration with peers were crucial tools to support quality assurance on projects, and on engineering solutions to roadblocks encountered to continue with primary data research collection digitally rather than in person.

In NHS quality improvement projects data collation in person was hindered, or meetings related to projects had to be rescheduled to meet the needs of the clinical service facing unprecedented demands. With workplace mentor agreement, students were then able to request access to online patient data captured on digital systems in a manner that sustained patient confidentiality, as alternatives to collecting in-person patient metrics. In some cases, entirely new projects had to be completed due to the pandemic pressures (they could not be carried out with respect to changing policy related to COVID-19). This was most likely experienced in other STEM-based research projects and may have led to impediments to project completion. By embedding quality assurance measures as above and working collaboratively with peers/mentors it can assist in identifying difficulties proactively, or reactively to then come up with plans to resolve glitches faced in action research projects/local research projects. It underscores the vitalness of ensuring research is viewed in line with the real world, and contemporary issues facing that particular discipline.

Before moving on to providing an action research project proposal and project an example blog to demonstrate the significance of maintaining quality assurance in teaching, and in revitalising course materials to make them more engaging and current will be shared. The blog was part of an assessment for the Subject Specialist Pedagogy (SSP) module for the level 7 postgraduate diploma in Education and Training. Note that the writing styles in blogs can be persuasive, a little more informal, personalised, and sometimes humorous, which differs to academic writing styles covered in Chapter 2.

Scrutinising the End of Unit Feedback Approach to Quality Checks for Course Updates and Revisions in Assessments for the Courses I Teach on?

For me this is a tricky feat as I am in my infancy in teaching. Following on from where I vehemently argued for the formative and summative assessments to be updated to typify the importance of helping to tackle antibiotic resistance, and modernise the mode of teaching delivered for the microbiology modules on the courses I teach on; how does one check for the quality in said renovation? I know a lot to consider in one breath and the title of the blog is a bit of a mouthful too, but moving on …

I will be evaluating the methods employed for quality checks on course innovation in the setting I work in. For online courses it is important that they unintentionally do not become too mass produced and be delivered primarily in a behaviourist fashion with sparse resources. For instance, such as too few tutors present to the number of students, and that the inbuilt online formative assessments become dull and encourage surface learning (Buitendijk, 2017). There is always the risk that students skip the learning materials on Ecordia, Moodle and Adobe Connect and head straight to the assessments, which they can then "google" the answers to. Given the current shortage of STEM teachers, there is a real risk of the ratio of teachers to students going towards too few tutors being available.

I will be focusing mainly on the level 4 microbiology course update in this blog. As a response to the concern mentioned earlier about students bypassing the module content I created formative assessments, where it was mandatory for the students to complete the further reading in the course materials to help prepare them for the summative assessments for the clinical modules. To improve student motivation with the tasks the students were encouraged to use websites that they may require in their future practice, and the assessment was contextualised as recommended by situated learning theorists (Stein, 1998). I am a great believer in this way of constructing assessments, and replicate this for my level 3, level 4, and undergraduate healthcare management and dissertation students. Further to this, students may need to shadow senior work colleagues as encouraged by social learning theorists such as Bandura. They may need to ask their colleagues for local workplace policies or ask for line manager/mentor input on a specific formative or summative task or seek advice on the research project they are doing whilst studying the course (Pajares, 2002). On Ecordia to facilitate mentor input from a senior work colleague, there is a tab where students can share a piece of work online for the mentor to provide advice on or comment on.

Supplementary to this the student is encouraged to complete self-directed study supporting andragogy-based principles of learning, through conducting research using the suggested reading provided or their own independent research on reputable resources that they have sourced (Huitt, 2009). This is important to encourage in the students, as it supports them in future CPD requirements as registered pharmacy professionals.

Below is an example task I created which represents aspects of the different learning theories, and wider skills advancement as mentioned above.

Now complete task 6. In this task for the setting you are currently working in, you have been asked to devise a workplace policy for contingency planning in case of an influenza pandemic. You will need to design a policy and upload it as an attachment. Use the website links for suggested reading in the plan to research this. Look at relevant workplace policies if available and do your own independent research to complete this task. The work needs to be Harvard referenced. Include the following points:

- How an influenza pandemic may occur?
- Mode of transmission, incubation period and infectious period.
- How a potential pandemic may affect your department, and strategies employed to minimise this?
- Contingency planning required.
- Hygiene measures suggested.
- The "at-risk" groups for whom post-exposure prophylaxis is recommended.

Suggested word count: 750–1000 words.

IT is embedded within the lesson task and the students' literacy and researcher skills are honed. This is advocated in the fourth Further Education Learning Technology Group (FELTAG) recommendation. Sector providers should have greater input in identifying, provisioning support, and moulding the digital skills and capabilities of learners. These skills developed can then be used in work settings (FELTAG, 2012). The task itself is something the students could be asked to do in a pharmacy organisation.

In the brand-new lesson, I have attempted to consider all the previously mentioned learning theories such as aspects of andragogy, social learning theory and situated learning theory and to promote IT skills development. Yet, it begs the question how do I know the students find it engaging? Are there any quality issues in the new lesson in achieving the wider skills growth? Does the new lesson meet the requirements for the current and future Pharmacy workforce?

These are haunting questions for me, because when I broached the subject with my peers, they advised me that the feedback from students is completed at the end of the unit being delivered. I have found that this is a major obstacle, due to it not allowing for modifications to be made in real time if there are any quality concerns with the updated lesson. This would mean that the student feedback can only be applied for the next cohort and not the current group. If a student voiced a genuine concern, then this would be a missed opportunity to intervene for the current group of learners. It impedes reflection in action, because the student voice isn't given a wholly sufficient platform to air their opinions, and viewpoints on the modules they are presently doing (Schön, 1983).

Reflection in action is an important feature in teaching practice and helps in improving the quality in teaching within real time. Furthermore, reflection in action to obstructions encountered in action research projects is again fundamental in improving teaching, and the infrastructure in place if a weakness is exposed in an educational establishment. This concept is critical to STEM-based research projects in practice.

My approach to help overcome this macro issue is to ask the other BTEC level 4 tutors for their feedback on the new microbiology lesson, and to review feedback requested from the students currently doing the microbiology lesson (a work in progress as not many students have started on unit 2 at present). This is a more proactive approach for quality checks in updates, which contrasts with the passive methods applied in the setting where end unit reviews are relied upon. The sample size would be small, because there are only a handful of students completing the new microbiology lesson at present and it limits the generalisation of the findings.

This is a genuine limitation in the approach; however, it is being treated as a pilot study. If further changes are required, then adjustments can be made before attempting this with a larger cohort (Ferrell et al., 2018).

Again, pilot reviews like this should be part and parcel of educational research. Inserting quality assurance mechanisms to determine the success of an intervention to improve outcomes should be reflected on keenly against theory supporting the innovation, and peer feedback. The feedback received from students and the other lecturers was positive in relation to the updated lesson. Most of the current students found the task engaging, and one quality issue was picked up. One of the links had expired, therefore I was able to find an alternative quite quickly for the current group to use and for subsequent cohorts of learners.

To help ensure quality in updates for online lessons, and to surmount potential threats as mentioned before learning analytics could be assimilated when reviewing student feedback to disseminate online academic learning and measure the degree of success and quality assurance in real time. Stretching this further, learning analytics can be used to inform teaching practice, and data streams could be used to provide illumination into how to make courses more in tune to real life to help overcome the central issues highlighted in this blog (Ferrell et al., 2018).

With any form of data acquisition and research including action research incorporating quality assurance measures at each stage is vital to minimise bias. It ensures good quality data is collected, that can potentially inform innovation in teaching pedagogy to benefit content delivery. Quality assurance mechanisms (through peer review) help to measure the degree of success in the interventions made in action research projects or in local research projects and can assist in maintaining impartiality. These could direct future recommendations with justification from the local evidence gathered. Embedding reflective practice and a collaborative approach can assist vastly in these areas and help navigate the growth of wider skillsets for learners to allow them to flourish in their future STEM careers! For two more personal examples of blog writing related to contemporary STEM teaching, visit the web pages below from the author website:

<https://stemlecturerjourney.wordpress.com/blog-1/>

<https://stemlecturerjourney.wordpress.com/blog-4/>

A free quiz can be accessed by readers of the book to test their knowledge on this chapter, by using a Smartphone to scan the following QR code or the readers can click the link below:

<https://forms.office.com/e/rEadQnAkW9?origin=lprLink>

Bibliography

Buitendijk, S. (2017) *Innovative Teaching for World Class Learning: Learning and Teaching Strategy*. [Online] Available from: <https://www.imperial.ac.uk/media/imperial-college/about/leadership-and-strategy/vp-education/public/LearningTeachingStrategy.pdf>. [Accessed 05 November 2022].

FELTAG. (2012) *FELTAG Recommendations*. [Online] Available from: <http://feltag.org.uk/wp-content/uploads/2012/01/FELTAG-REPORT-FINAL.pdf>. [Accessed 03 November 2022].

Ferrell, G., Smith, R., and Knight, S. (2018) *Designing Learning and Assessment in a Digital Age*. [Online] Available from: <https://www.jisc.ac.uk/guides/designing-learning-and-assessment-in-a-digital-age>. [Accessed 24 August 2024].

Huitt, W. (2009) *Humanism and Open Education*. [Online] Available from: <https://www.edpsycinteractive.org/topics/affect/humed.html>. [Accessed 12 April 2023].

Pajares, F. (2002) *Overview of Social Cognitive Theory and of Self-efficacy*. [Online] Available from: <https://people.wku.edu/richard.miller/banduratheory.pdf>. [Accessed 22 October 2022].

Schön, D. (1983) *The Reflective Practitioner*. San Francisco: Jossey-Bass.

Stein, D. (1998) *Situated Learning in Adult Education*. [Online] Available from: <https://eric.ed.gov/?id=ED418250>. [Accessed 26 August 2024].

CHAPTER 6

An Example of a Research Proposal

Introduction

In this chapter the focus is on research proposal construction (elements such as the research topic practicalities, setting aims and objectives, inserting quality assurance mechanisms, methodology choices, sample size, related ethics and possible obstacles and timescales will be covered). A research proposal from own STEM teaching experience is included overleaf to delve deeper into these aforementioned areas. The research was completed as part of the Level 7 postgraduate diploma in education and training course. In the action research project, the main aim was to assess the successfulness in applying the newly created novel academic writing/Harvard referencing task at course induction in addressing the lack of academic writing proficiency observed in student work. These were new tools designed by the lecturer to help students get used to academic writing early in the course, to improve the quality of the student summative assessments being submitted. This action research project was being approached from the second cycle.

Marrying up national and global frameworks outlined in earlier chapters with local action research for teachers (ECT, trainees, and established) could assist in a customised approach to research in line with wider guidance. By ensuring structures are in place to enable effective action research with sufficient funding, this could be a means of having better quality targeted initiatives to improve regional student achievement levels where low attainment levels are observed whilst aiding teacher retention. It shares elements of a SoTL approach discussed in the introduction of the book. In the West Yorkshire FE setting a significant number of students enrolled on the course were found to have English as their second or third language or were from a lower socio-economic background. Most exhibited weak academic writing skills as they had only studied to level 2 previously. By reviewing these student demographics and reflecting under the autobiographical lens, the lecturer developed a dynamic class-wide approach to promote academic writing skills growth. This encompassed a first-person action research approach in the first cycle of action research completed, prior to the second round of action research detailed overleaf in the action research proposal (Hartney, 2020).

Principle 12 of the Global Professional Teaching Standards framework strongly backs the notion of using action research in a profound manner to develop students to their full potential where:

> Governments and education authorities have an obligation to ensure that teachers receive the necessary support, training, professional development, opportunity to engage in and access research, including action research to enable all students to develop to their full potential. (Education International and UNESCO, 2022)

The new teaching interventions constituted examining and reflecting on this issue to create an academic writing/Harvard referencing task to supplement this area of learning for STEM students using learning theories and concepts such as adaptive teaching, learning analytics and CLR principles (discussed in earlier chapters).

In the second cycle of action research, it was primarily concerned with quality assurance and assessing the Harvard referencing/academic writing tasks under the four different perspectives as per Brookfield's lenses. Aspects such as learning analytics and combining this with other learning theories are articulated to help determine the success of the intervention. The principle focus of the action research project was on the second cycle of research to build on the first cycle of action research. The application of reflection under different perspectives, and adapted learning analytics was used to assess the level of success with the novel approaches created in supporting academic writing skills development from the first cycle, and on whether any further improvements could be made in the second cycle. See below a copy of the Action Research Proposal:

Action Research Proposal Exemplar

School of Teaching, Health & Care

Teacher as a Researcher Proposal Form

Student: Saba Ahmed
Enrolment No.: 10605973
Course: Level 7 PG Diploma in Education and Training (In service)

Supervisor: xxxxx xxxxxxx xxxxxx

Proposed Title of Research Project

Using augmented learning analytics and contemporary learning theories to assess new academic writing resources, and to investigate whether further adaptations are needed?

Purpose of Research Aims and Objectives

To determine the success (quality assurance check) of the recent application of adaptive teaching, and CLR in improving academic writing standards for learners on this STEM course.

Identify if there are any further areas of improvement for the recently updated induction referencing/academic writing resources?

To determine whether taking a more innovative humanism-based, and adaptive teaching approach helps in the quality of student assignment work completed compared to previous groups?

This will be determined by using two strategies as described below:

1) By using lecturer feedback to gauge this. Lecturer feedback will be obtained via completion of questionnaires and semi-structured interviews.
2) To check the quality of the novel academic writing task from the student perspective, this will be accomplished via the use of on-line student reflective accounts submitted on Moodle (capturing the learning analytics dimension). For task 2 of the new academic writing/Harvard referencing task, the learners in the level 3 classroom cohort will complete a reflective account in the induction task. If any students raise any interesting points in the reflective accounts, then semi-structured interviews or a forum will be used to probe these points further. Student data will remain confidential and anonymity will be maintained. The findings may inform improvements on the task for future groups.

Background/context of the research

Previously there was assignment writing guidance, which the students were asked to read alongside example assignments, and it detailed how to correctly reference work in accordance with the Harvard referencing system employed in the FE education establishment in West Yorkshire. As per feedback from informal lecturer standardisation meetings on the BTEC level 3 and 4 courses it has been perceived that there is a universal issue of incorrect or lack of referencing in work, which emerges in student assignments resulting in a high number of resubmissions.

Fact-checking and verifying work for STEM learner assessments is crucial. These are evidence-orientated fields, therefore students evidencing independent researcher skills and academic writing skills to showcase a wide breadth of reputable resources have been consulted are important for both the course and in their future careers. Many professionals based in STEM disciplines will come across queries or could be asked to develop policies. Having a firm grasp of evidence types, and methodical academic writing and researcher skills are fundamental abilities to be able to carry out these tasks effectively.

When completing feedback for student assignment work across both courses, this in most cases is a developmental feedback point included. After having discussions informally with other lecturers, there is a shared consensus on this; therefore, aspects of learning analytics, learning theories, adaptive teaching and CLR are being used to gain advancements in the areas requiring improvement (CLR, n.d.). Upon reflection some students may not read the assignment writing guidance nor the example assignments, and perhaps just engage with the assignment work. This could be attributed to many reasons such as not having a task set to test whether resources were read, or the resources are lacklustre for students to engage with.

As a result of the feedback from students and from personal teaching experience to date ideas were formulated to remedy this by creating a short induction task for the students to complete an academic piece of writing, with correct in-text citations and references in line with Harvard referencing. In the new innovative task, they have useful websites and a live lesson for further guidance on this area. Assignment writing guidance is provided. The students need to read a personal example of a short piece of academically written work to assist them in structuring their work and assist them with future summative assessments for the course. The Harvard referencing/academic writing skills induction research task promotes self-directed skills, and independent researcher skills enhancement (a copy of the plan is included in Appendix 1).

The online links below are used to support them with assignment writing, independent research, and Harvard referencing:
<https://library.bradfordcollege.ac.uk/Referencing>
<https://library.bradfordcollege.ac.uk/studyskills>

After reading all the resources the students must write a short 500–600-word assignment researching a minimum of three different reputable sources on a topic related to pharmacy/healthcare that they are interested in, with correct in-text citations and referenced as per the Harvard referencing system used at the college. They can access external resources (website links included above) to support them with the referencing element of their written work. The aim is that by including a variety of resources, and by making the task more relatable it caters to different types of learners, whether they are more visual or auditory learners etc., and it makes it more engaging for them (Roell, 2019). The task is designed to support independent researcher skills development.

Alongside this the student will be tasked to complete a reflective account on this piece of work and what they found the most enjoyable with it, anything new that they have learnt and what they thought could be improved? After analysis of the reflective accounts in conjunction with their short pieces of written work either focus groups or semi-structured informal interviews will be carried out to capture greater elaboration on specific points, which require expansion to determine if there are further enrichments that can be made to the academic writing tasks. This primary data acquired will be more qualitative in nature. The strategy of mostly qualitative methods to discern the quality of the novel induction task has been selected to help ensure the student voice is not neglected. This perspective can be valuable in measuring the quality of the learning tools created, and where aspects could be improved upon for future cohorts. Some quantitative data will be extracted.

The academic writing skills task, and reflective accounts have been approved by the course leads to include in the induction tasks for students on both the level 3 and 4 courses following informal peer discussions. This exemplifies a somewhat CLR approach (CLR, n.d.). The research project is being approached from the second round of action research and embodies second-person action research. A cyclical approach to research assists in continually improving areas, and in preventing complacency. It will allow quality assurance to be measured for the novel tasks created, and possibly inform future enhancements.

Proposed sample group

By 21 October 2019, the entire level 3 classroom group will be used as the sample, and their academic writing tasks including their reflective accounts will be evaluated. One entire cohort has been selected rather than a cross-section from the different groups, because it can allow deeper examination in one group. All three groups cannot be analysed due to the sheer number of students as there would be over 200, and in the timescale provided this would not be achievable to do as per advice from the research project supervisor. The importance of reflecting on supervisor feedback on research projects is depicted here, because this was only a 3-month project. Reviewing 200 plus student reflective accounts, alongside the other methods of data acquisition would be a tall order in such a limited timescale.

By 5 November 2019, the two other level 3 course lecturers in the organisation will complete the lecturer questionnaires, to ascertain how successful colleagues felt the academic writing skills task was in improving this years' student assignment work in comparison to previous years. A mixture of open and closed questions, and questions with scales are being used in the tutor questionnaire. Some of the data gained here will allow for quantitative dissemination, and part of the data will be qualitative. Semi-structured interviews will be used to extract richer information and allow more in-depth analysis to enable further exploration of key points raised in the questionnaires. For the two level 4 BTEC course lecturers this will not be possible, as the unit 1 assignment deadline dates for the current level 4 cohort is after the submission deadline date of this action research project. Their feedback is still valuable, so they will be asked to complete the first three questions of the questionnaire by 15 October 2019, but the level 3 course lecturers will complete the additional two questions by 5 November 2019. All four lecturers will complete the first three questions in the questionnaire by 15 October 2019.

Methodology

As stated above the use of online reflective accounts will be used to establish the student perspective on whether an improvement in their academic writing skills has occurred from the new interventions, resulting from the first action research cycle. This will be mostly qualitative in nature. The entire classroom level 3 cohort will be the sample, and via email consent forms will be sent out to each student. This is to ensure that they are fully informed of the purposes of this research and understand that their data will not be misused. It will notify students that any information from their reflective accounts, and work completed will remain anonymous to protect their confidentiality. The proposed merits of the research project will be incorporated too for both the lecturer and student consent forms.

Extending the dissemination of the reflective accounts further, they will be assessed for any common patterns, recommendations, and any negative elements, which will then be compared against any secondary research already published in this area by 5 December 2019.

With the informal lecturer interviews and lecturer questionnaires (this includes questions which have scales, therefore the data acquired will be partly numerical and for the open questions this will provide qualitative data). Scrutiny of the mixed data will help audit the quality of the newly designed academic writing skills task, and on whether colleagues found that it improved the quality of the students' work in contrast to previous years (to acquire a before and after of the new interventions). In this way a partial CLR approach under the peer lens alongside learning analytics, and adaptive teaching strategies to inform future adaptations to support learning with academic writing skills development can be achieved (CLR, n.d.).

The primary research methodologies resemble a mixed research methodology, where both quantitative and qualitative data collation methods will be employed to evaluate the research topic. Methodological triangulation is being used where multiple data sets are being examined (student data and lecturer data), and multiple methods such as questionnaires, reflective accounts, and semi-structured interviews are being used to gain as much insight as possible in a short timeframe. In addition to this, a narrative literature review will be conducted to ascertain deeper probing in teaching strategies to improve academic writing skills (Bell, 2005).

In terms of gaining appreciation from secondary data already published a narrative literature review will be completed. The research published in this area is not overly abundant, and a narrative review has been selected for this reason to gain a broad perspective on the impact of educational institutions supporting academic writing skills advancement. Rather than applying filters such as making it specific to Harvard referencing, which neglect other referencing styles such as APA (American Psychological Association). A less restricted approach is being used to ensure relevant studies on developing academic writing skills and referencing that could be useful to the action research project are not discounted from the small pool of research available. A summary of the reported literature will be conveyed on key elements uncovered. This could inform further enhancements to back interventions to support academic writing skills growth in STEM students, which could be implemented in the local FE organisation. It could provide other discernments (Coventry University, n.d.). It will help acquire a more detailed appreciation under the theoretical perspective.

Methods of Data Collection

A mixture of student reflective accounts, lecturer questionnaires and semi-structured interviews (possibly focus groups) will be employed to enable qualitative and quantitative data acquisition. Also, a literature review will be conducted as above. For the narrative literature review key phrases such as "academic writing skills and formative assessments", "educational interventions and referencing

> styles", "wider literacy skills", and "learning theories and literacy skills" will be used in Google Scholar searches to obtain a volume of literature published in the field.
>
> All researchers (including students) have the responsibility to respect the rights and dignity of research participants. This is particularly important when conducting research with vulnerable groups in society such as children.
>
> All researchers must maintain high ethical standards and respect and protect the participants in their research.
>
> Guidance can be sought from British Psychological Society (BPS), British Educational Research Association (BERA), Social Research Association (SRA) and other relevant professional bodies.

Use the following boxes and headings to identify how you intend to deal with ethical issues which may be encountered in your research.

> ## Protection of Participants
>
> All participants must be actively protected from any form of harm; this may be emotional, intellectual, or physical.
>
> The students and course lecturers will be fully briefed on the purposes of the research, and to protect them steps will be taken to ensure that the data collated will be anonymised fully.
>
> This study has a minute potential risk of harm, due to careful diligence in both the design of the task and in the methodologies selected in the study with due consideration allocated to safeguarding parameters as well.
>
> No personal information is being obtained. The data will be anonymised to maintain student confidentiality.

The Right to Withdraw

All participants must be aware that they have the right to withdraw from the research at any time.

Within the consent form this will be made explicit to the students and lecturers.

Confidentiality

All data must remain confidential. Everyone has the same right to privacy, including vulnerable groups for whom confidentiality as an issue is even more crucial.

The action research project will be conducted in line with the relevant xxxxxx College policies and GDPR (General Data Protection Regulation), as per the current UK Data Protection laws (Data Protection Act, 2018).

Informed Consent

The researcher must explain as fully as possible the aims and purpose of the research so that participants can give *informed consent*. How the information will be used and who will have access to the research must also be explained. Participants must not be *deceived* in any way about the nature and use of the research.

It will be made clear that the information is only to be used anonymously as part of the action research project with their confidentiality protected. They will be informed that the purposes are to direct own teaching practice. The research will be used to identify the degree of success with the novel interventions, and in identifying any areas of improvement for the academic writing skills task. These areas will be assessed through the application of learning analytics, and a deep reflection combined with a CLR approach. This will be using their reflective accounts and short pieces of written work.

The same principles and purposes apply for gaining the peer perspective for the lecturers, who may choose to participate in the study.

Consequences and Benefits

The researcher must be able to justify any research by showing how the positive benefits outweigh any negative consequences to participants.

The research is to inform local teaching practice, and potential benefits for the learners and future cohorts on the course. It will give both the students and fellow course lecturers a platform to provide feedback on the success of the novel academic writing skills task; therefore, they could potentially shape any improvements or tweaks for future cohorts. It promotes a democratic approach to learning. There is little risk to the students, as there is nothing they will be asked to do, which is outside the scope of these courses. The work is not linked to a final grade, therefore all parties involved can be assured that the risks are minimal. The rewards for driving forward improvements and determining the quality of the novel task set are much greater though.

Another benefit could be that more reflective accounts are set for students in the future, so it could inspire students to take charge of any further learning they would like to consider supporting future CPD requirements. This encourages lifelong learning, as reinforced in standard 4 of the GPhC standards, "maintain, develop, and use their professional knowledge and skills" (GPhC, 2024). In essence reflective learning could be furthered on the course.

An Example of a Research Proposal

> ## Specific Ethical Issues relating to this Research
>
> To protect confidentiality, all data will be anonymised to work in line with ethics related to research, and to work in line with legislation mentioned previously related to personal data and confidentiality.

When planning a research proposal, it is important to consider feasibility for the research idea and to reflect keenly right from the start of the project. It is pragmatic to have a backup idea, in case the first idea for a research project is not realistic to complete. Deliberate on the practicalities for the specified research. In the research proposal it should include background reading to examine secondary data already published. This helps apprise the research proposal with an evidence base behind it. Reflect under the autobiographical lens and local trends/patterns too. Thoughtfully reflect on different methodologies to make explicit the reasons for the choice of methodology as per the individual research project and connect it to contemporary learning theories and concepts. Furnish justification for the choices in your research methodology and design. As always ethics need to be duly mulled over, and so does maintaining privacy and confidentiality throughout the research project. Having a co-operative approach to research is critical to identify issues such as making the research too big for the time allocated. Fortunately, due to discussing the project proposal with the research project supervisor the researcher was able to reflect and make changes to the project proposal to sidestep this pitfall. As an extension by gaining feedback from the mentor and peers, this highlights the potential for the ITTECF framework to be expanded on to use peer support in second-person action research for trainee teachers to pin down issues and collaborate with other teaching professionals that are more experienced to improve learner outcomes (DFE, 2024).

The real-life example of a project proposal highlights how research proposals can be constructed in a holistic, objective, and practical manner, which embraces different viewpoints to counter any potential issues. This research proposal serves as a strong example for local/action research projects that trainee teachers are completing particularly in STEM education, which considers the current landscape and contemporary issues. Before moving onto the next chapter the following web page from the author website provides a useful summary on action research:

<https://stemlecturerjourney.wordpress.com/action-research-stem-education/>

A free quiz can be accessed by readers of the book to test their knowledge on this chapter, by using a Smartphone to scan the following QR code or the readers can click the link below:

<https://forms.office.com/e/C5GC9hqaBM?origin=lprLink>

Bibliography

Bell, J. (2005) *Doing your Research Project.* 4th edn. Suffolk: Open University Press.

CLR. (n.d.) *Collaborative Lesson Research UK.* [Online] Available from: <https://www.collaborative-lesson-research.uk/>. [Accessed 08 June 2023].

Coventry University. (n.d.) *Narrative Literature Reviews.* [Online] Available from: <https://www.futurelearn.com/info/courses/systematic-literature-review/0/steps/89025>. [Accessed 31 December 2023].

Data Protection Act (2018). [Online] Available from: <https://www.gov.uk/data-protection#:~:text=The%20Data%20Protection%20Act%202018%20is%20the%20UK's%20implementation%20of,used%20fairly%2C%20lawfully%20and%20transparently>. [Accessed 10 March 2024].

Department for Education. (2024) *Initial Teacher Training and Early Career Framework.* [Online] Available from: <https://www.gov.uk/government/publications/initial-teacher-training-and-early-career-framework>. [Accessed 26 August 2024].

Education International and UNESCO. (2022) *Global Framework of Professional Teaching Standards.* [Online] Available from: <https://www.ei-ie.org/en/item/25734:global-framework-of-professional-teaching-standards>. [Accessed 24 August 2024].

GPhC. (2024) *Standards for Pharmacy Professionals.* [Online] Available from: <https://www.pharmacyregulation.org/pharmacists/standards-and-guidance-pharmacy-professionals/standards-pharmacy-professionals>. [Accessed 24 August 2024].

Roell, K. (2019) *The Visual Learning Style.* [Online] Available from: <https://www.thoughtco.com/visual-learning-style-3212062>. [Accessed 26 August 2024].

CHAPTER 7

An Exemplar STEM Lecturer Action Research Project

Introduction

In this chapter a full action research project report will be shared from the introduction right through to the conclusion/recommendations to illustrate how research principles combined with reflection, and action research can help improve teaching practice in a specific area. In different education settings the most pressing issue may be entirely different. In another setting it could be that vaping in young children is the issue, or the most urgent concern is to improve numeracy skills in the organisation, or it could be classroom behaviour management that needs addressing. The methods used and research study design would be unique to that topic area under investigation.

If the example of the rise in the number of young children vaping is taken, this may warrant student questionnaires for data collation to identify the number of students vaping in the education establishment. Focus groups could be held to gain the student perspective on how to help tackle the issue. It may require partnership with other organisations such as local NHS organisations to support students to quit vaping, or from starting it in the first place. The research methodology would be mainly primary data collation methods. Student questionnaires could yield quantitative data on the number of vapers at the education establishment, and to assess the level of success with the interventions implemented. On the other hand, focus groups (qualitative data) could be held to gather opinions to further inform ways to help students quit vaping. In the literature review secondary research methodologies would be required to provide an evidence base to back the interventions being chosen.

Vaping is thought to be a safer alternative. It is a useful aid to quit smoking however in children who have never smoked before, due to it being perceived as "being cool" younger children with no smoking history are taking this up. Vaping is considered to be safer than smoking (although it is not absent of all risk) and could exacerbate respiratory conditions such as asthma (NHS Digital, 2022). By working with other organisations, it could provide an avenue of support to access services to help students quit vaping. Strategies could be engineered to prevent children from taking it up in the first place through education.

For all research projects keep quality assurance, and the aims and objectives at the heart of research projects. Take steps to minimise researcher bias and pre-empt potential problems from occurring in the first place. Keep an open mind too, as research project outcomes could be surprising.

Grassroots research projects in any STEM discipline are extremely important. These skills should be sharpened at undergraduate level. If not, it could diminish the STEM practitioner propensity to carry out impactful research, and tackle issues in an evidence-based practical approach in their future field.

Again, the research methodology, and research project design may differ in the approaches used. The ambition is that an example action research project report from start to completion is of use to all researchers to make clear the applications and implications of research principles. It builds on concepts and themes explored in the previous chapters, and revisits these with a full action research project report to make research principles connect more with readers of the book. In this chapter it will present justification on the choice of methodology/methodologies as per the research topic under investigation, and why other methodologies in the primary and secondary research methods were discounted. The action research project also serves as an example of an academically written piece of work to exemplify how academic writing differentiates from reflective writing (reflective writing is covered in Chapter 2 of this book). An example of a blog has been supplied in Chapter 5.

Note that the action research project is conducted on a small scale, therefore the findings are not generalisable. The action research project report itself demonstrates elementary research principles in practice (see next).

Using Augmented Learning Analytics and Contemporary Learning Theories to Assess New Academic Writing Resources and to Investigate Whether Further Adaptations Are Needed?

Abstract

Introduction

For many students in FE and HE settings there is a longstanding issue of weak academic writing. To surmount this issue a novel task was created after undertaking a deep reflection using the Brookfield's critical lenses. Yet a second issue arose after the first cycle of action research, which was how to measure the quality of the academic writing skills task in achieving its' aims? This was the central theme for the second cycle of action research.

Aim

To retrospectively analyse whether the task led to significant gains in academic writing in the FE setting by applying the Brookfield's critical lenses to learning analytics, to measure the quality of the task. To investigate whether teaching interventions predicated in adaptive teaching, and CLR elements to fortify academic writing skills for students led to improvements?

Methods

Across a two-month period between October 2019–December 2019 the task was applied to fifteen students on the BTEC level 3 Diploma in Pharmaceutical Science. All four components of the Brookfield's critical lenses were analysed to help acquire a rich and meaningful reflection, and specifically a revised approach to learning analytics was used to obtain the student perspective.

Results

All fifteen students found the task useful to assist with academic writing, and five students made further comments on how to improve the referencing task. All four academic lecturers found the task very useful in improving academic writing standards and commented that there were marked improvements in assignment-level work.

Conclusion

The novel academic writing skills task rooted in humanism principles and constructivism with teacher-led interventions that had a CLR focus and adaptive teaching elements, supported the findings in secondary research that using multiple resources aided in making sizeable advances in student academic writing (Mandernach et al., 2016). Although further fine-tuning was necessary to improve the academic writing/Harvard referencing induction tasks.

Table of Contents

> Introduction
> Narrative Literature Review
> Methodology
> Results
> Results Discussion
> Conclusion/Further Recommendations
> Bibliography

Introduction

Creating the New Referencing Task

Using the self-critical lens underperformances were observed in the majority of student assignment work across the course. This was in terms of academic writing skills, independent research, sentence structure, grammar, punctuation, completion of in-text citations and writing in line with the Harvard referencing system employed at the local FE establishment. Taking a class wide approach in areas, which need advancing such as on literacy skills, academic writing and referencing promotes high standards for all learners. It aligns with standard 5 of the ITTECF (DFE, 2024). This shows the benefits of an adaptive teaching approach (adaptive teaching is covered in the introduction). Secondary research supports inadequacies being observed in student coursework (Landrum, 2013, cited in Mandernach et al., 2016).

This initial reflection permitted an inspection to be undertaken under different angles. It was the first cycle of action research, which resembled the characteristics of first-person action research (Hartney, 2020). A unique task on academic writing was produced, where the students would have to write in line with the Harvard referencing system after researching a minimum of three reputable resources, and the students needed to complete a reflective account to encourage them to contemplate further self-directed study.

Context for the Second Cycle of Action Research

After creating the task, it led to further questions:
How can the success or lack of success in classroom-wide interventions typifying traits of adaptive teaching, and humanism blended with constructivism elements in course materials be discerned?
How can quality assurance be assessed?

Aims and Objectives

Hence a second cycle of action research was completed with the broad aim of ascertaining the quality of the task in achieving improvements in student academic writing. It resulted in harnessing the Brookfield's critical lenses, with the use of learning analytics as quality assurance tools for the course update.

- To use the Brookfield's critical lenses in tandem with learning analytics, and a CLR approach to acquire a weightier understanding of the good elements of the

updated approach in improving academic writing skills. Qualitative and quantitative methods were used to assesses this.
- To identify if there were any further areas of improvement for the recently updated induction referencing/academic writing resources?
- Reflecting under the autobiographical lens to inform updates required.
- To determine whether taking a more innovative humanism based, and adaptive teaching approach helped improve the quality of student assignment work submitted compared to previous groups (by reflecting under the student and peer lenses)?
- Acquiring an appreciation under the theoretical lens, by completing a narrative review of the topic area under investigation.

Narrative Literature Review

Learning analytics as defined by the "Horizon Report" published in 2006 is using web analytics to aid learner profiling and gathering data on levels of student engagement with online learning tasks (Johnson et al., 2016). The Brookfield's reflective model was used in an adjusted approach to learning analytics to serve as a quality assurance measure for the new task. It diverges from commercial learning analytics tools available because this modification to learning analytics allows for more substantial largely qualitative data to be acquired on the issue from online student reflective accounts. Rather than analysing the number of times a student attempts a quiz online, there was a deeper exploration gained with the amended learning analytics strategy used (Ferrell et al., 2018). The significance of using deep not surface-level reflection to improve teaching practice retrospectively is supported in the concept of "Reflection on action" coined by Schön and advocated in other literature published (Burns and Bullman, 2000, cited in Nottingham University, 2009).

Moreover, secondary research in this area shows that students using other referencing styles in their academic written assessments, such as the APA (American Psychological Association) also exemplify errors in writing (Landrum, 2013, cited in Mandernach et al., 2016).

The writers Luttrell et al. (2010) concur with the tactic of using multiple resources to enhance standards in academic writing within introductory, and even higher education level courses. Using this method is optimal in educational practice because it cultivates student fluency in improving the quality of writing with the correct referencing style used at that particular education provider. Class-wide approaches to boosting advancements in different teaching areas for instance literacy skills, or other areas using adaptive teaching is encouraged (DFE, 2024).

For students to develop academic writing skills in these areas scaffolding as advanced in constructivism-based learning theories was considered, where the task included online resources to assist all the students to complete a short piece of academic writing on a topic of their choosing within Pharmacy/wider healthcare (Scales, 2008). To help foster student-centred learning and encourage independent learning, this task was purposefully designed so the student could select their own topic. By allowing the student choice in what they could write about it supported a humanism approach to learning and andragogy as put forward by Knowles (1975), due to it encouraging self-directed study for adult learners. This is vital for the students as they will one day become registered pharmacy technicians. To maintain registration, they must meet CPD (continual professional development) requirements underpinned in the GPhC standards for Pharmacy professionals (GPhC, 2024).

This strategy shares characteristics with heutagogy principles related to learning, which advocate the use of constructivism and humanism amongst other learning theories to encourage lifelong self-determined learning (Blashke and Hase, 2016).

Some authors such as Hartley (2009) as cited by Williams et al., (2014) argue that there is an obstacle to teaching referencing and given the difficulties this should be taught in the second year. Others would argue that this is something that students should be completing at the start of a course, as it takes time to refine literacy and researcher skills (Lamptey and Atta-Obeng, 2012). Also, by revisiting an important area of learning repeatedly as recommended in the spiral curriculum (branching from cognitivism) by authors such as Bruner (n.d., cited by Johnston 2012), this could vastly improve academic writing proficiency in student assignment work. Furthermore, it emphasises the imperativeness of fact-checking in a scientific discipline.

Within the local Yorkshire FE setting the use of learning analytics is in its' infancy and is an area requiring betterment. It can be integral to inform us what works well, and what needs altering for future cohorts as supported by secondary research completed in this area (Ferrell et al., 2018). The current quality assurance checks at the local FE setting are paper-based and are completed at the end of the academic year. They cover the modules and not the induction work. Additional to this if students are carrying out reviews at the end of the year, they will most likely forget what they have done at the start of the year (Ferrell et al., 2018).

Ruminating under the autobiographical lens within pharmacy, there are more structured quality checks on clinical pharmacy services delivery through completion of clinical audits periodically. This supports clinical governance and helps to ensure patient safety is kept paramount (NHS Improvement, 2018).

Action research within education can be used as a mechanism to investigate, and research a new intervention to improve teaching practice on a concern/issue identified (both at the same time). It can be cyclical in nature where you must acclimatise continuously, and re-audit/investigate multiple times to gauge the success or lack of success of an approach within personal teaching practice (Cohen and Manion, 1994, cited in Bell 2005, p. 8).

Within the action research project multiple methods were used to gain a wealth of information on the application of quality assurance measures to determine the success of the task, alongside examining secondary research published in this area.

Methodology

The data acquisition was mostly qualitative in nature with some quantitative data. This multi-method approach to data collation is otherwise known as triangulation (Laws, 2003, cited in Bell 2005, p. 116). For the student perspective the methods included evaluation of online student reflective accounts with the use of semi-structured interviews to investigate key points, which students raised in their reflective accounts. This is a useful way to ensure the student voice is heard using a digital platform, with the use of learning analytics amongst other methods to inform course improvements (Ferrell et al., 2018). It allowed for the student perspective in the Brookfield's reflective model (1995) to be reviewed.

The variables were controlled, where the same task was applied to all students, after they were briefed collectively to ensure reliability and validity of results. Augmented learning analytics via assessment of student reflective accounts was analysed in conjunction, with peer feedback from other lecturers to support aspects of a CLR approach. The peer perspective data collation methods included lecturer questionnaires with closed and open questions (the questions with numerical scales permitted quantitative data to be gathered, and the semi-structured interviews allowed qualitative data acquisition). This mixed research methodology approach was used to inform future adaptive teaching strategies to improve academic writing skills. Using the idea of reflective accounts to promote a student-centred approach to learning endorses self-directed skills growth for learners too.

The students were tasked with completing an academic piece of writing after conducting research using a minimum of three reputable sources, and ensuring Harvard referencing conventions were met. This helped in comprehending the level of skills for students in these areas. As this induction task was being trialled for all students in the class for the first time, it was important to gain feedback from different parties to ensure a rich reflection was accrued. The peer feedback was gained from questionnaires and interviews, and the student feedback was gauged using online reflective accounts on the task (a modified approach to learning analytics). Furthermore, the theoretical perspective was appreciated in the narrative literature review. The narrative literature review was used to capture a summary of similar studies and allowed for published information to be analysed including other concepts such as applicable learning theories and learning analytics.

A systematic review would have been more specific, and a meta-analysis could assist in better statistical analysis. Those options may have led to relevant studies, and other literature being omitted. This was not appropriate because of the limited pool of research available. Systematic reviews and meta-analysis or scoping literature reviews may be more apt for many other studies though. A narrative literature review in this case allowed for a broader perspective to be realised (Coventry University, n.d.).

Analysis under the autobiographical lens occurred through the lecturer assessing previous student assignment work, and in lesson observations where the weakness in academic writing and researcher skills was noticed.

Potentially some may argue that there was no control group, and for primary research in the medicine field the gold standard would be randomised controlled trials (RCTs). Yet the principles of RCTs in terms of having one placebo group/control group, where there is no intervention and one group having an intervention meant this was discounted. This would be a very controversial and unethical approach to an educational study design, as there would have been a lack of opportunity for one group and all students should be given a fair and equal chance to develop their literacy skills (UNICEF, n.d.)

The sample size was fifteen for the students as one student did not want to take part, because they had included sensitive information on a relative (case study) as part of the academic written work submitted. Supplementary to these three semi-structured interviews were completed with students in this cohort.

Some numerical data was extracted alongside mainly qualitative data. This was used to inform adaptive teaching strategies and garner a partial CLR approach to academic writing skills advancement.

Key Legislation and Ethical Considerations

A mixture of different methods to acquire both qualitative and quantitative data was implemented, therefore ethical facets needed to be considered carefully. Student work was analysed therefore care was taken to ensure this was anonymised, and valid consent was obtained. This is in line with the BERA Ethical Guidelines for Ethical Research (2011) and the ESRC Framework for Research Ethics (2012). Both underscore the Research Ethics policy at the local FE establishment, where the action research project was conducted in West Yorkshire (Messam and Stevens, 2017).

In the modern world personal data is prone to data mining, and measures needed to be taken to prevent repeat occurrences of recent controversies such as the Facebook scandal occurring. The infamous Cambridge Analytica scandal, as reported in the Guardian online by Wong (2019), highlights the exigency of ensuring that data is used ethically, and for the purpose that consent has been provided for. This was made clear in the consent forms for both students, and course tutors participating in the research that their data would be kept secure and confidential.

To eliminate unconscious bias and to protect the confidentiality of the students participating in the semi-structured interviews, a fellow course lecturer was asked to scribe the student responses, as opposed to recording the information within a classroom where other students could overhear the responses or the lecturer doing this themselves.

Normally, researchers would argue for mainly quantitative data as it is deemed to be more reliable; however, qualitative data method acquisition allows for richer exploration to be achieved and is more tailored to the individual. In this situation more in depth knowledge was required to ascertain the opinions of different parties therefore qualitative data was more appropriate to use with some quantitative data.

In the next section results will be analysed and evaluated to see how they can enlighten possible future improvements, and in assessing the success of the task. Again, these results will be scrutinised under the four lenses of the Brookfield's lenses.

Results/Results Discussion

From reviewing the results table above, it can be determined that 100% of the students found this work useful. Two students (13.33%) commented specifically that they found the online resources were useful, and five students (33.33%) made suggestions on areas where the task could be improved. In terms of students (66.66%) not making any further comments on improvements or that they found the task needed no further improvements, this could be credited to students not feeling confident enough to speak up. This is observed in secondary research where the student voice

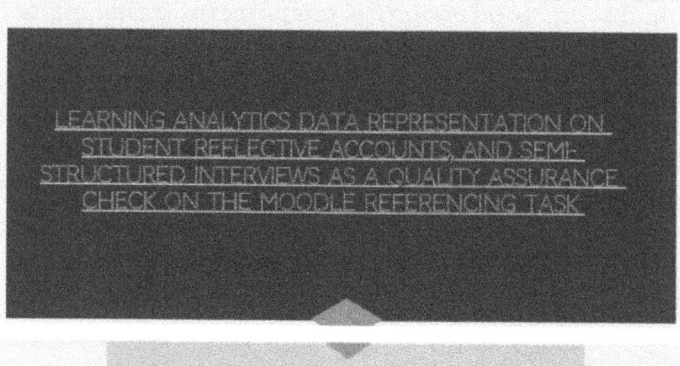
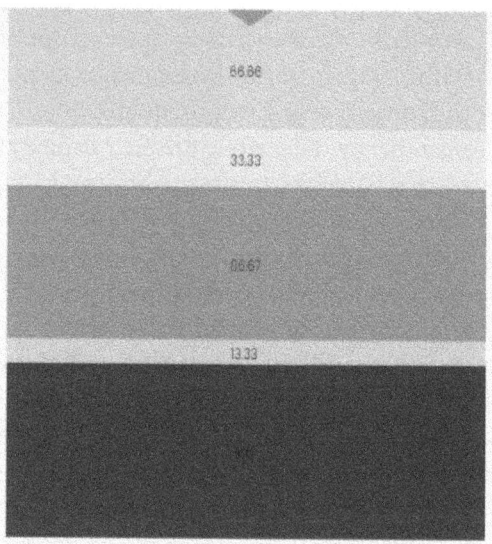

Figure 4. Learning Analytics Student Reflective Accounts Data

Table 1. Results on Student Reflective Accounts

Number of students who found the task useful for academic writing:	15
Number of students who found the resources useful:	2
Number of students who made no comment on the online resources included in the task:	13
Number of students who made comments on how to improve the task:	5
Number of students who felt no further improvements were required or did not make any comments for further improvements:	10

may be given a platform, however not all students feel at ease to use this in fear that they may displease their academic tutors/lecturers (Ferrell et al., 2018).

Students upon completing their reflective accounts provided the following positive comments as seen in Figure 5.

By evaluating this mostly qualitative data from the student reflective account comments, it has been ascertained that all the students found the task useful. Some students were introduced to a whole new style of writing. By having practice at this, they are now equipped to use this for their future assignment work. This is key for lecturers to foster, where students should be given constructive feedforward in their feedback to grow their academic writing skills. Establishing that it is a learning curve for students is quite important to make students feel less pressured with assignments, and thus less student anxiety is experienced with essays. Student anxiety with assignments cannot be wholly eliminated. If students feel too stressed, then this may hamper progress in academic writing proficiency, and maturation in researcher skills.

Moreover, from the comments provided on the online reflective accounts (augmented learning analytics) completed by the students, it

Student Comments on the Moodle Referencing Task

"After completing the short essay on the waste of medicine in the medical environment, I was able to not only improve on my ability to write, learnt references and refresh my mind-set from working in a pharmacy to a learning environment".

"I felt the task of referencing quite straightforward, the format in which to reference evidence was easy to follow and believe it has helped me feel more confident when completing assignments in future".

"As I haven't used referencing in a long time, I found this very challenging. However I feel as though I am gaining more knowledge on this now and am eager to do more in order to improve".

" I really enjoyed learning about the Harvard referencing style and executing it to the best of my ability".

" I think this task went very well, however I think I need to work on my referencing".

" I found the task really useful as I haven't done referencing in a few years".

"Researching an unknown topic and being able to gain knowledge from it has been the best part of the task".

"Referencing is fairly new to me so it was nice to be able to practice the skills taught in the induction session at college".

"Overall I enjoyed this assignment, because I gained new knowledge of drug addiction; I was introduced to new vocabulary and style of writing".

Figure 5. Examples of Student Reflective Accounts Comments

can be discerned that they were motivated with completing the task that was revamped to make it more engaging with the use of contemporary theories as described earlier. By using elements of constructivism blended with aspects of humanism, it has allowed some students to acquire a more self-determined outlook on learning not only new topics but to enhance their academic writing skills adeptness as well. This self-determined learning is advocated in heutagogy principles (Blashke and Hase, 2016).

Semi-structured Interviews Qualitative Data Analysis

For three of the five students who made specific suggestions on improving the task in the student reflective accounts; semi-structured interviews were completed to probe key insights. Investigating the insights in more depth helped improve the academic writing skills task for the next cohort. The fourth student was late to start the course therefore they submitted the task 1 work and reflective account quite late, so there was not enough time to complete a semi-structured interview for this student. The first student was absent on the day these semi-structured interviews were conducted with the students. As there was a short timescale to complete the action research project more time could not be spent on the data acquisition component hence only three students were interviewed.

Student 1: "I would have liked to be provided with a topic to research." The student was absent on the week the semi-structured interviews were conducted; therefore, they were unavailable to interview. Nonetheless the comment was explored under the theoretical viewpoint. The initial aim was to keep the task as open ended as possible and not to restrict the student. Upon reflection this may have meant too much choice was available. This could pose an obstacle to some students. Some students may not be able to pinpoint, which topic to pick due to cognitive overload (CESE, 2017). Cognitive load theory asserts that in our working memory there is the capacity to hold nine or ten pieces of information roughly, therefore within the task perhaps there was too much content to sift through (just with the sheer choice available). Upon further analysis from the theoretical lens of the Brookfield's reflective model the RAS (reticular activating system), and cognitive load theory can interplay to affect student learning. Some students could be overwhelmed with researching different topics and find it difficult to narrow down what to write about. It could be challenging for the filtering effects of the RAS in the brain to take place effectively (Study Academy, n.d.). A way of overcoming this is by listing example topics that the students could research to provide focus for some students who don't know where to start, but still leave it open-ended in order not to restrict other learners who prefer independent learning and more choice (Huitt, 2009).

Student 2: "I think the only thing that could be done to improve the task is writing to a command word, as I personally find it quite difficult to know when to stop writing when a specific objective isn't laid out." A command word/verb was not used when designing the novel task, due to the underlying ambition of supporting personal choice and using a more humanism-orientated strategy to teaching. This builds on the suggestion made by the first student, where a resurging theme is being observed. Some students wanted more focus on the task. Upon completing the interview with this student, they expanded that they would like to have had a mixture of command verbs. By providing possible topic suggestions with the inclusion of different command verbs it could facilitate more effective learning for those students who would prefer more structure in the academic writing skills task. Yet by providing an option for the student to choose their own topic, this would not be stifling to those learners who prefer self-directed study and more choice.

With humanism-focused teaching there are drawbacks such as too many choices available. Some students may not be inclined to learn best this way, as they may require more structure with command verbs and learning objectives as promoted in behaviourism (Scales, 2008).

Student 3: "Personally, I would prefer to reflect on the piece of work (and write this statement) after it has been marked and I have some feedback, although I appreciate that now the work is fresh in my mind so I can think about it in greater detail." This comment in the reflective account was something that warranted further investigation; therefore, this student was selected for a semi-structured interview to gain a deeper appreciation of the student perspective.

They explained in the interview, "I wasn't sure if I had completed the academic piece of writing correctly or incorrectly, so I couldn't reflect on the positive and negative aspects of the tutor feedback." To ensure the student perspective is factored in from the adapted application of learning analytics the students could do this in week one of the induction, to improve the delivery of this task. This means the students have sufficient time to complete the work, receive feedback, and then in week two they can complete the reflective accounts with the tutor feedback to hand. By amending the timing of the task, and the approach in this manner it could allow students time to reflect on their first piece of feedback on academic writing. They could use this as feedforward to help them to complete their first assignment. To a degree this resonates with experiential learning as advocated by writers such as Kolb, where reflection is key to learning (Gravells, 2014, p. 44).

Reflecting using the theoretical lens further it has been viewed that students in HE settings show significant levels of dissatisfaction with feedback from their lecturers, and course tutors as reported in the 2005

National Student Survey. Poor quality feedback could stagnate the growth of students. By providing good quality feedback, which is constructive, as highlighted by Race (2007) in his influential "Ripple in the Pond Theory", it could vastly improve the understanding a student has on a particular topic area. More developmental feedback for students in all module assessments is key.

Student 4: "I did find it tricky to stay within the 500–600-word limit, as I could have gone into all the different pharmacological reasons as to why the drugs were addictive, as well as being more in-depth with the symptoms of withdrawal playing a part for patients addicted to opioid drugs." This was another good developmental aspect raised by a student. A 500–600-word count was nominated with this being an induction task, but the student wanted a larger word count. Within the semi-structured interview, the student provided further detail on the main reason for this where they mentioned, "As the students can touch on more points". Possibly the word count could be extended to 700–800 words. Although with it being an induction task and there only being limited time to complete the work, this may not be realistic for students to do in the time allotted.

Student 5: "It would have been more helpful if there was something about referencing books, or other sources of information as I feel like that is not something many people including myself know how to do." This student started later therefore they could not be interviewed. They had limited time to complete the work, because their first few assignments were due around the same time. Subsequently the student may have missed the resources and links provided which had this information. They were signposted to these in the feedback provided.

Lecturer Questionnaires Results

All lecturers on the BTEC level 3 and 4 courses found the task very useful for their students. Before the task was applied, lecturers had informal suggestions to make alterations to the task before it went live on the level 3 classroom cohort such as on the word count. Some suggested 1,000 words, and others suggested 500 words. It was decided that 500–600 words were appropriate due to it being an induction task.

After the task was applied the two BTEC level 3 course lecturers were invited to observe a live lesson on Harvard referencing and academic writing. They were selected to provide responses for the remaining questions on the questionnaire. This has allowed for the peer perspective, and partial CLR approach to be realised under the Brookfield's reflective model. From their responses even though the sample size was quite small, rich qualitative data was acquired.

By working in a collaborative fashion in the local education establishment the creation, and implementation of the task has led to other lecturers on the level 3 course using this as a blueprint to create the assignment for unit A/1 on health and safety and safeguarding as depicted in lecturer commentary in Figure 8. It adds weight to the usefulness of having a partial CLR approach, where there is a potential for good practice to be shared post-implementation of an adapted lesson task to support learning amongst a community of teachers. Not only this but the lecturer's feedback on assignment work is showing that students are improving in their independent research skills by using reputable sources, which is an immensely important attribute for scientific disciplines and other disciplines. This notion is strongly supported in the FELTAG report published in 2012, to advance for students. It was a privilege to have the opportunity to share best practice like this with other departments, and members of the teaching team. It is action research like this that can forge strong student academic and researcher skills. It can help equip students in STEM disciplines to complete impactful local research in their future practice.

Conclusion & Recommendations

By adapting the way academic writing and referencing is taught on the course, it progressively tackled the deficits seen in academic writing in student assignment work in a positive manner. Having multiple resources and using adaptive teaching strategies informed by CLR approaches, and learning analytics using the Brookfield's lenses to support students in academic writing was beneficial to improving this area (DFE, 2024; CLR, n.d.). Using interventions to improve academic writing standards in

An Exemplar STEM Lecturer Action Research Project

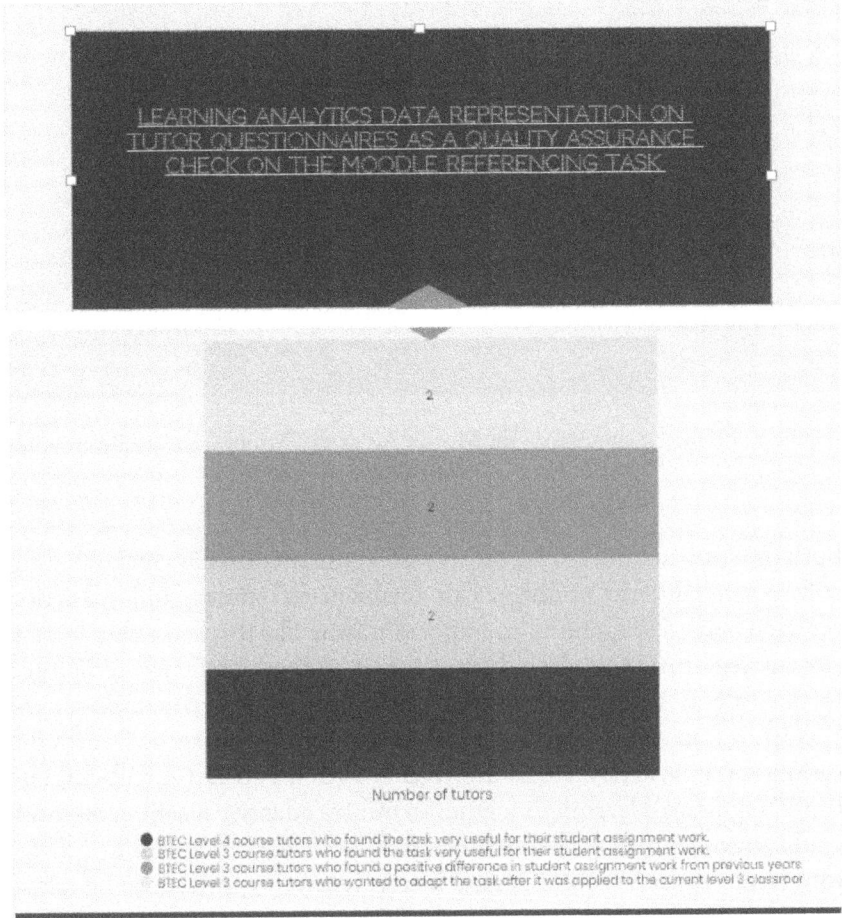

Figure 6. Lecturer Questionnaire Data for the Academic Writing Skills/Harvard Referencing Task

student work is a shared consensus observed in secondary research published too (Mandernach et al., 2016). Rather than just reflecting under one perspective a more holistic methodology, and deeper reflection assisted more profoundly in making further tweaks that were useful to improve academic writing standards for STEM learners. The sample sizes for

> **Tutor Comments on the Moodle Referencing Task**
>
> 'This is an immensely useful task that is backed up with sound and solid information regarding referencing. This skill is very important for our students – it's required for their academic studies particularly their assignments. They will require this skills for future studies, especially HE courses'.
>
> 'This is a fantastic task that helps to set the students up for their actual assignments. Academic writing is a skill which is lacking in a lot of the first year students and this task gives them an opportunity to learn these skill prior to submissions'.
>
> 'I think this task is very useful to students as it prepares them for assignment writing. I haven't completed any further learning since my BTEC L3 and I imagine this is the same for most students and I feel this task is not only useful for referencing, but also a reminder to producing a written piece of work'.
>
> 'It is an excellent way to start developing your academic written skills at level 4 and see what may be potential developmental areas for example, referencing and in-text quotations'.

Figure 7. Lecturer comments on the Moodle Academic Writing/Harvard Referencing Skills Task

both the students and course tutors were quite small, which makes it difficult to generalise the findings. This amalgamated strategy in local action research helped to examine an important issue like this at a richer level as per the region, and student demographics to then manufacture tailored tactics to enrich academic writing skills proficiency further. Under the ITTECF framework mentor input is strongly encouraged. Local education research/action research projects with a partial CLR focus, and use of augmented learning analytics to inform adaptive teaching methods could engender beneficial outcomes in different areas that require growth too. It allows for a second-person action research approach to be taken, when CLR principles are used in the action research project.

Applying the Brookfield's reflective model with learning analytics helped to discern the quality of the task from different perspectives. After analysing the qualitative and quantitative data it was affirmed that the task has improved the quality of student academic writing. This was echoed in the data acquired for both the classroom student cohort and lecturers sampled. Additionally, by using different vantage points such as the autobiographical lens, the student lens (to ensure the student voice wasn't neglected), the peer lens and finally the theoretical lens, it allowed judgements to be made on where further enhancements could be made for the

Tutor follows up questionnaire responses after the Academic Writing/Referencing Task was applied to the level 3 cohorts

1. In comparison to past student assignment work how has the referencing element to your feedback provided to students differed?

    Tutor 1 response:

    "My feedback to students now contains less feedback on referencing. In fact, my feedback now contains positive encouraging words about the level of referencing in assignments. The students have been able to produce far better academic quality work by actively researching for sources as a means of referencing it, in doing so they have discovered a wealth of information on the topic being assessed."

    Tutor 2 response:

    "I am having to comment less on the use of referencing in the learners' assignments. The work submitted has consistently formatted assignments in regards to how the references are included i.e. in text citations and complete bibliography."

2. At this stage would you adapt the tasks in any way?

    Tutor 1 response:

    "The task is clear as is. In terms of adaptation, I would possibly add to the task to include operative verbs such as describe, evaluate etc., so that the students can gauge their work."

    Tutor 2 response:

    "With the new qualification I think this task could be adapted to be the first assignment for unit A/1. This unit covers the basics of safeguarding, and health and safety in the workplace. This would be a nice easy assignment to get students used to academic writing."

3. Have you used it in any other way to develop the course further and if yes how?

    Tutor 1 response:

    "We are currently using it in the induction process. However, we are planning on using this task at a slightly earlier stage so that the students can receive their feedback well before they actually work on their summative assignments. Earlier feedback- positive encouragement to students reinforces their abilities and room for improvements from constructive feedback. Use the task in combination with learning styles questionnaire- this would help students among other things to find their best way of learning at an earlier stage."

> Tutor 2 response:
> "I have just used it as the initial induction task however I believe it should be integrated into the SOW to be done by every cohort of students."

Figure 8. Lecturer Responses for the Remaining Questions on the Lecturer Questionnaires

task. The future enhancements suggested were to include example topic areas with operational verbs and learning objectives (as advanced in behaviourism), and more step-up scaffolding for some students as recommended in constructivism-orientated learning theories (Scales, 2008).

Another area for the second part of the task that was identified as an area to adjust under the autobiographical and peer lens was to incorporate a reflective model, or choice of reflective model for the reflective accounts (to further advance heutagogy principles). This recommendation could assist in equipping learners with tools to encourage self-directed learning, for them to take charge of their own learning to develop further as reflective practitioners. These areas can be ignored in STEM disciplines, but most STEM fields have a reflective component. They require a self-directed focus to support lifelong CPD. Encouraging reflective practice wherever possible in STEM courses is crucial for learners.

Another potential use of student reflective accounts could be to complete online reflective accounts on all the modules undertaken on the course to aid quality assurance in real time (Nottingham University, n.d.). Using learning analytics, this could serve as an extra quality assurance check for other course updates. The current quality assurance checks take place at the end of the year. Doing them at periodic intervals and online could assist in determining what has gone well with the teaching, and where improvements could be made to propel course improvements for subsequent cohorts and for the current group.

There are wider issues rather than just at the grassroots level, which should be redressed. One such issue is that there is a lack of FE research in this area. It is estimated that approximately 10 per cent of young adults within the UK hold other postsecondary qualifications such as diplomas, and approximately 20 per cent of these are termed as low-skilled in literacy or numeracy or within both areas (Kuczera et al., 2016). Perhaps if more

FE academic action research was conducted in this area, there could be more done to overcome this and improve the academic writing skills for BTEC students and T Level students.

Another underlying reason for weak academic writing for the BTEC level 3 course could be attributed to the actual curriculum framework learning outcomes, where there is hardly any emphasis placed on referencing and independent researcher skills advancement (GPhC, 2017).

By sharing this action research project in full, it established the importance of using peer discussions with mentors and inviting mentors to observe different interventions used by those new to teaching. It was an instrumental tool in serving a dual purpose, of helping to source valuable expertise to support early career teachers (ECTs), and in enabling effective quality assurance measures through peer review and feedback. Adding in some form of action research/local research for ECTs, or for those undertaking teacher training could help counteract the disconnect with national agendas and what is actually happening in reality. Utilising reflection under the four different Brookfield's lenses (self, peer, theoretical and student perspectives), and linking this with contemporary learning theories assisted the researcher to undertake an impactful action research project. Positives were accrued in academic writing and researcher skills development for STEM learners (DFE, 2024; Education International and UNESCO, 2022).

Action research coupled with fair funding for teaching as per local educational needs, and prominence being awarded to professional development could all go hand in hand to help ameliorate and offer solutions to the pressures and obstacles faced by teaching staff. In turn specific strategies could be customised as per issues faced within their own setting. This may help to encourage retention for both new and experienced teaching staff within all education settings, because the teacher practitioner has greater professional autonomy, and there is an effective framework in place to enhance teaching pedagogy to innovate and overcome a particular issue or issues. This approach is advocated within principle 12 underpinning the Professional Standards Framework from the joint EI/UNESCO framework. For all action research projects/local research projects it is immensely vital to consider ethics, maintaining confidentiality for the participants, and to mull over the contemporary issues impacting practice.

To sum up on a local level working collaboratively with other lecturers (partial CLR approach) and using a multi-method approach to improve adaptive teaching on academic writing has led to some elevations in this area of weak academic writing skills. Although there are wider macro issues persisting. By combatting the underlying reasons for teacher strikes and using resources adequately whilst promoting action research as one potential tool to reduce regional variations in educational attainment levels; this could improve the learner journey, and educator experience alike. Both the macro and micro level need to be reformed, therefore local action research projects should be aligned to relevant parts of national and international frameworks in education alongside local policies to address the concerns within that region.

The job is not done, and in teaching no two cohorts are ever the same. By using adaptive teaching, elements of CLR and learning analytics combined with learning theories in the action research project, this was essential in making improvements to lesson materials and lesson delivery for academic writing in own practice to support learners. However, more improvements may be needed in future. Embracing the cyclical nature of research is key!

By sharing this example of an action research project, with a strong STEM orientation, it emphasised the potential positive gains that can be made with local research in education. The simple and straightforward manner that research principles and terminology were presented in this chapter, hopefully is of value to all researchers to help demystify research principles and see the benefits to practice of mixed methodology approaches to data collation. It illustrates the merits of conducting a secondary literature review, and the hope is that it explained when some options are not suitable to use in research projects too. The example action research report may support readers in formatting their own research project reports.

A free quiz can be accessed by readers of the book to test their knowledge on this chapter, by using a Smartphone to scan the following QR code or the readers can click the link below:

<https://forms.office.com/e/yn73eqdyRd?origin=lprLink>

Bibliography

Bell, J. (2005) *Doing Your Research Project*. 4th edn. Suffolk: Open University Press.

Blashke, L. M., and Hase, S. (2016) Chapter 2: A Holistic Framework for Creating Twenty-First Century Self-Determined Learners. In B. Gros, Kinshuk., and M. Maina (eds), *The Future of Ubiquitous Learning Designs for Emerging Pedagogies*. Berlin: Springer-Verlag, pp. 25–40.

CESE. (2017) *Cognitive Load Theory in Practice*. [Online] Available from: <https://education.nsw.gov.au/content/dam/main-education/about-us/educational-data/cese/2017-cognitive-load-theory.pdf>. [Accessed 25 August 2024].

CLR. (n.d.) *Collaborative Lesson Research UK*. [Online] Available from: <https://www.collaborative-lesson-research.uk/>. [Accessed 08 June 2023].

Coventry University. (n.d.) *Narrative Literature Reviews*. [Online] Available from: <https://www.futurelearn.com/info/courses/systematic-literature-review/0/steps/89025>. [Accessed 31 December 2023].

Department for Education. (2024) *Initial Teacher Training and Early Career Framework*. [Online] Available from: <https://www.gov.uk/government/publications/initial-teacher-training-and-early-career-framework>. [Accessed 26 August 2024].

Education International and UNESCO. (2022) *Global Framework of Professional Teaching Standards*. [Online] Available from: <https://www.ei-ie.org/en/item/25734:global-framework-of-professional-teaching-standards>. [Accessed 01 July 2023].

FELTAG. (2012) *FELTAG Recommendations*. [Online] Available from: <http://feltag.org.uk/wp-content/uploads/2012/01/FELTAG-REPORT-FINAL.pdf>. [Accessed 05 November 2022].

Ferrell, G., Smith, R., and Knight, S. (2018) *Designing Learning and Assessment in a Digital Age*. [Online] Available from: <https://www.jisc.ac.uk/guides/designing-learning-and-assessment-in-a-digital-age>. [Accessed 22 November 2022].

GPhC. (2024) *Standards for Pharmacy Professionals*. [Online] Available from: <https://www.pharmacyregulation.org/pharmacists/standards-and-guidance-pharmacy-professionals/standards-pharmacy-professionals>. [Accessed 24 August 2024].

GPhC. (2017) *Standards for the Initial Education and Training for Pharmacy Technicians*. [Online] Available from: <https://www.pharmacyregulation.org/students-and-trainees/pharmacy-technician-education-and-training>. [Accessed 24 August 2024].

Gravells, A. (2014) *The Award in Education and Training*. London: SAGE.

Hartney, E. (2020) *Action Research in the midst of COVID-19*. [Online] Available from: <https://www.royalroads.ca/sls/action-research-midst-covid-19>. [Accessed 07 March 2024].

Huitt, W. (2009) *Humanism and Open Education*. [Online] Available from: <https://www.edpsycinteractive.org/topics/affect/humed.html>. [Accessed 12 April 2023].

Johnston, H. (2012) *The Spiral Curriculum*. [Online] Available from: <https://files.eric.ed.gov/fulltext/ED538282.pdf>. [Accessed 02 November 2022]

Johnson, L., Adams Becker, S., Cummins, M., Estrada, V., Freeman, A., and Hall, C. (2016) *NMC: Horizon Report 2016 Higher Education Edition*. Austin, TX: The New Media Consortium.

Knowles, M. S. (1975) *Self-Directed Learning. A Guide for Learners and Teachers*. Englewood Cliffs: Prentice Hall/Cambridge.

Kuczera, M., Field, S., and Windisch, H. C. (2016) *Building Skills for All: A Review of England*. [Online] Available from: <https://skillspanorama.cedefop.europa.eu/en/useful_resources/building-skills-all-review-england.> [Accessed 05 November 2022].

Lamptey, R. B., and Atta-Obeng, H. (2012) Challenges with Reference Citations among Postgraduate Students at the Kwame Nkrumah University of Science and Technology Kumasi Ghana. *Journal of Science and Technology*, 32(3), pp. 69–80.

Luttrell, V. R., Bufkin, J. L., Eastman, V. J. and Miller, R. (2010) Teaching scientific writing: Measuring student learning in an interactive APA skills course. *Teaching of Psychology*, 37, pp. 193–195.

Mandernach, J. B., Zafonte, M., and Taylor, C. (2016) Instructional Strategies to Improve College Students' APA Style Writing. *International Journal of Teaching and Learning in Higher Education*, 27(3), pp. 407–412.

Messam, S., and Stevens, G. (2017) *Research Ethics Policy*. Bradford: Bradford College.

NHS Improvement. (2018) *Safety, Clinical Audit and Clinical Governance during Major Change*. [Online] Available from: <https://improvement.nhs.uk/resources/safety-clinical-audit-and-clinical-governance-during-major-change/>. [Accessed 02 November 2022].

NHS Digital. (2022) *Decrease in Smoking and Drug Use among School Children but Increase in Vaping, New Report Shows*. [Online] Available from: <https://digital.nhs.uk/news/feed/?r56_r1:page=5&r56_r1:pageSize=10>. [Accessed 03 November 2022].

Nottingham University. (n.d.) *Reflection on Action*. [Online] Available from: <https://www.nottingham.ac.uk/nmp/sonet/rlos/placs/critical_reflection/origins/reflection_on_action.html>. [Accessed 23 November 2022].

Race, P. (2007) *The Lecturer's Toolkit*. 3rd edn. Oxon: Routledge.

Scales, P. (2008) *Teaching in the Lifelong Learning Sector*. Maidenhead: Open University Press.

Study Academy.com. (n.d.) *Reticular Activating System: Definition and Function*. [Online] Available from: <https://study.com/academy/lesson/reticular-activating-system-definition-function.html>. [Accessed 04 November 2022].

UNICEF. (n.d.) *Randomised Controlled Trials (RCTs)*. [Online] Available from: <https://www.unicef-irc.org/KM/IE/impact_7.php>. [Accessed 02 October 2022].

Williams, G. J., Emerson, A., Larkin, R. F., and Norman, C. (2014) Four Activities to Promote Student Engagement with Referencing Skills. *Psychology Teaching Review*, 20(1), pp. 90–95.

Wong, J. C. (2019) *The Cambridge Analytics Scandal Changed the World – but It Didn't Change Facebook*. [Online] Available from: <https://www.theguardian.com/technology/2019/mar/17/the-cambridge-analytica-scandal-changed-the-world-but-it-didnt-change-facebook>. [Accessed 03 October 2022].

CHAPTER 8

The Virtues of Developing the Grassroots Researcher/Action Researcher for Future STEM Practice

Introduction

In the final chapter some personal examples of local research/action research completed in own pharmacy practice will be supplied. The main aim of these projects was to improve local health outcomes. If the researcher doesn't have skills developed at an undergraduate level, then the future STEM professional will lack the necessary researcher skills to complete meaningful local action research in their STEM discipline.

By detailing different examples of grassroots research, this will evidence how local research is fundamental to practice especially for STEM professionals. This is why teaching on STEM courses needs to facilitate proficient researcher skills growth for students enrolled on these types of courses.

Teaching should never be viewed in isolation from the real world, and current practice. Firm associations with the world of work need to be maintained to make the learning on STEM courses more accessible, and award prominence to maturing researcher skillsets. If students can't observe the real-world applications of knowledge or research skills being taught, then this could easily lead to disengagement.

Local Antibiotic Prescribing Audit

Introduction & Background

A local STEM action research project in a clinical setting needed to be completed, where a clinical audit was undertaken to monitor the levels of compliance of antibiotic prescribing for doctors and nurses, in line with local primary care guidelines within the Yorkshire locality. The local primary care guidelines were an essential tool to ensure antibiotics were being prescribed correctly; however, the local guidelines weren't always being followed. Some prescribers were deviating from them.

The apt and correct use of antibiotics is essential in treating infections, and in reducing the risks of antibiotic resistance. There are a finite number of antibiotics with not many new antibiotics coming into market, and the correctly targeted use of antibiotics is necessary to ensure these lifesaving drugs will remain effective for future generations for as long as possible. Local guidelines include first-, second-, and third-line options for a particular type of infection. This strategy ensures coverage against the most likely causative micro-organism culprit, whilst also factoring in local antibiotic resistance rates. In cases where lab reports such as sputum culture results show that first-, second-, and third-line options are ineffective due to antibiotic resistance, then specialist microbiology advice should be sought (Leeds Teaching Hospital NHS Trust, 2019).

Methodology

As part of the local STEM research project an audit was created (to assess the level of deviation), and then use it to inform interventions to promote working in line with local primary care guidelines when prescribing antibiotics. Elements of the first-person and second-person action research were utilised, where the researcher was creating a training package as they were completing the audit (they kept adding to it as more and more discrepancies came to light). The training package under development was shared with senior colleagues to provide peer feedback/review to improve the local prescribing of antibiotics in line with local guidelines. After the audit was concluded the training package was finalised, with sign off from department leads.

This was a prime example from personal STEM professional practice of running a clinical audit to assess compliance rates of prescribers using local antibiotic protocols, and to create an intervention (training package) to support the local prescribers. It fundamentally evidences the importance of moulding researcher and literacy skills at undergraduate level, as STEM professionals including pharmacy professionals may need to undertake research projects or conduct audits as part of their future STEM practice. A research topic/question was posed to assess this, and the methodology included running drug searches on antibiotics as part of the audit (metronidazole, amoxicillin, doxycycline, cefalexin, phenoxymethylpenicillin, trimethoprim, nitrofurantoin etc.). It helped compile a list of patients that were prescribed these antibiotics on EMIS, to establish the sampling frame/pool. EMIS is a computer program that is used in GP settings widely.

Interval sampling was used in the internal audit to select every tenth patient prescribed each of these antibiotics in the last 6 months to determine if antibiotics were being correctly prescribed as per local protocols, and that the antibiotic prescription was necessary by examining patient notes retrospectively. The research methodology was quantitative. The results were carefully analysed, and patient details were anonymised to comply with the Data Protection Act (2018). In essence interval sampling is where subjects are selected at a fixed interval, and the sample is acquired in a manner where researcher bias is minimised (Elfil and Negida, 2017).

Results & Results Discussion

Overall, the prescribing of antibiotics was mostly in line with local formulary guidelines, with a score of roughly 75 per cent accuracy with antibiotic prescribing for the audit. Errors occurred on the length of prescribing for certain infections. Another common error was the use of antibiotic options such as trimethoprim in the Leeds area routinely. This was unsuitable due to resistance rates being estimated to be 30 per cent or greater in the locality at the time (this may have risen from 2019) (Leeds Teaching Hospital NHS Trust, 2019). This was attributed to a gap in knowledge for prescribers on local resistance rates for trimethoprim, which is an antibiotic used for urinary tract infections (UTIs). The audit provided an ample opportunity to present this to the board and finalise the training package to support prescribers. NICE national guidelines (2018) advocate trimethoprim or nitrofurantoin as first line options if a woman is not pregnant or for use in males. Within this locality this should not have been prescribed first line, because of the higher antibiotic resistance rates associated with trimethoprim in this area contrasted against other localities.

Another interesting case was the prescribing of cefotaxime in a UTI infection, and this was most likely in error. Cefalexin is an option to prescribe second line. A discussion took place with the prescriber to signpost them to the local prescribing protocols for UTIs. Both antibiotics sound similar, which may have contributed to the error.

Conclusion

Antibiotic resistance is on the rise, and therefore apt prescribing of antibiotics is a necessity to keep them effective for as long as possible. Research is ongoing; therefore, the audit was repeated in 6 months to assess if the training package led to improvements. Improvements were achieved with antibiotic prescribing in line with local guidelines to roughly 96 per cent. To further enhance prudent prescribing of antibiotics in the prescribing team the researcher arranged further training with a microbiology pharmacist, to help improve prescribing for UTIs in line with local protocols and to reflect local secondary data on antibiotic resistance rates.

Local STEM action research like this is imperative in improving outcomes, and in mitigating the risk of antibiotic resistance as much as is possible. Possessing a strong appreciation of research principles, and scrutinising data published with a critical thinking cap on is useful. These are the cornerstones of making improvements in STEM disciplines, and in conducting primary grassroots STEM research. Exploring local STEM action research in conjunction with lab reports, peers and wider national or local guidance is fundamental to manufacturing strategies to propel advances forward in the area being researched.

Not having researcher skillsets buoyed from completing an undergraduate-level research project would have left the researcher without the expertise and skills to conduct grassroots research like this in a STEM field. They would have been less capable of making a progressive impact on judicious antibiotic prescribing in their local area.

Quality Improvement Project on Smoking Cessation

The next example to be shared of local STEM action research is from a former pharmacy technician studying on the BTEC level 4 course, who was completing a quality improvement project for smoking cessation in their setting. It uncovered a massive gap in smoking cessation services in their region. The research methodology was mixed where they used questionnaires with closed questions (quantitative patient data degenerated), and open questions (to gather qualitative patient data). They attended stakeholder meetings to improve their own understanding of smoking cessation services in their area. In one of the meetings, they realised that in their area there was no connecting hospital smoking discharge service with primary care community pharmacies and GP settings, when patients were discharged back into the community from hospital. The action research project the pharmacy technician was doing evolved to reflect this, and she was instrumental in designing this part of the service in her locality, to help improve access to smoking cessation services for patients. In turn aiding continuity of care between primary care and secondary care settings.

Engineering STEM Research Example

Extending this further with a contemporary engineering example is the failure to replace asbestos in schools up and down the country, which has been the cause of death of hundreds of teachers. This is more concentrated in the north. It is local research like this, which can uncover regional disparities to help make recommendations that are essential to improve building work (Thames Laboratories, 2023). Local research projects are essential in garnering improvements in areas, and in identifying facets with shortfalls in practice in many STEM disciplines.

As portrayed with these local STEM action research/local research project examples local research requires a good grasp of research principles, strong problem-solving abilities, and robust critical analysis skills. Breaking down these research principles and highlighting how research can potentially lead to improvements in STEM practice is paramount in enhancing the researcher skillsets in these areas for students enrolled on STEM courses. Relaying across the practical real-world applications of research is essential for teaching on undergraduate STEM courses.

By sharing these local examples of grassroots research in Chapters 7 and 8, the prominence of developing undergraduate STEM student researcher skills has been demonstrated. Honing researcher skills and promoting a deeper appreciation of research principles on STEM courses for students are precious commodities in furthering progression for future STEM professionals in their careers as supported in principle 3 of the joint EI/UNESCO framework (Education International and UNESCO, 2022). It will assist them in identifying areas that have fissures.

The issues unearthed could be small, or highly significant dependent on the findings. By developing problem-solving skills and collaborative working skills; such skills can then be applied to craft solutions to make improvements in a wide range of real-world situations. If these skills are neglected on STEM courses, then it is a disservice to students enrolled on the courses, because they won't be able to achieve a deeper comprehension of researcher skills and the applications to practice. This could impact them adversely in their future STEM practice, where they could be ill prepared

The Virtues of Developing the Grassroots Researcher

for working in practice. This chapter establishes the importance of boosting these critical wider skills. It buttresses the notion that teaching should not be viewed in a vacuum, and to promote STEM student researcher skills development by establishing concrete links in teaching with contemporary issues in STEM disciplines. Otherwise, they may be less equipped to complete local STEM research/action research in their own practice, when required to do so in their future careers.

A free quiz can be accessed by readers of the book to test their knowledge on this chapter, by using a Smartphone to scan the following QR code or the readers can click the link below:

<https://forms.office.com/e/dd2UkiNZvc?origin=lprLink>

To review further examples of the applications of learning theories, coupled with action research (see the link below for the author website). The website contains more practical examples, reflective accounts and blogs from the STEM lecturer experience to further expand key concepts covered in the book.

<https://stemlecturerjourney.wordpress.com/>

Bibliography

Data Protection Act (2018). [Online] Available from: <https://www.gov.uk/data-protection#:~:text=The%20Data%20Protection%20Act%202018%20is%20the%20UK's%20implementation%20of,used%20fairly%2C%20lawfully%20and%20transparently>. [Accessed 10 March 2024].

Elfil, M., and Negida, A. (2017) Sampling Methods in Clinical Research; an Educational Review. *Emerg (Tehran)*, [Online] 5(1), pp. 1–3. Available from: <https://www.ncbi.nlm.nih.gov/pmc/articles/PMC5325924/>. [Accessed 01 October 2023].

Leeds Teaching Hospitals NHS Trust. (2019) *Women with Lower Urinary Tract Infection (UTI) in Primary Care.* [Online] Available from: <https://www.leedsformulary.nhs.uk/chaptersSubDetails.asp?FormularySectionID=5&SubSectionRef=05.01.13&SubSectionID=A100#3958>. [Accessed 24 August 2024].

NICE. (2018) *UTI (Lower): Antimicrobial Prescribing.* [Online] Available from: <https://www.nice.org.uk/guidance/ng109>. [Accessed 12 March 2024].

Thames Laboratories. (2023) *Map of "Cancer Causing" Schools Shows Horror Time-Bomb.* [Online] Available from: <thameslabs.co.uk>. [Accessed 07 June 2023].

Afterword

In this book the pertinent reasoning behind action research combined with reflection, collaborative practice, the wider context, and exploration of theory to help drive course improvements forward in teacher action research projects have been conveyed. Hopefully the research principles surveyed will furnish a refresher for all budding researchers. The differences between academic writing and reflective writing were highlighted. With the use of written examples readers have blueprints for these writing styles to help them in structuring their own research reports, and reflective accounts. The quality of different types of published evidence was covered as well. Complex research terminology such as systematic reviews, literature reviews and meta-analysis were demystified. The importance of multifaceted approaches in ensuring quality assurance is maintained in research projects, and using action research as a means of enabling progressions in areas of learning provision exhibiting deficiencies locally have been explored.

Extending the benefits of research, and learning analytics combined with contemporary learning theories such as adaptive teaching and CLR, it can be observed that sometimes in the initial cycle of research system desired levels of improvements may not occur. Though on the next cycle where further adaptations are made, these can facilitate more pronounced advances in teaching practice and learner achievement.

Local action research like this should be encouraged in FE and HE settings, and learning from projects like these should be cascaded to different regions to share good practice. There is a potential for greater research in educational settings to help with staff retention issues as more autonomous teaching practice is fostered that could enable career progression, and a fresh outlook can be realised on how to support students if there are any areas of concerns (Kay, 2020).

A link for the article published on my action research project in the national publication TES can be accessed in Appendix 2 (TES membership is required to access this).

Critical to enhancing teaching pedagogy is reflection under different viewpoints to ensure a holistic approach is taken. Supporting critical research skills development and self-directed learning can help empower students in any course discipline. Rich reflections can be transformative and empower teachers to promote reflexivity approaches in their students whilst simultaneously helping to advance own careers as teaching professionals. Research coupled with collaboration with peers and reflective practice could improve standards in weaker areas and encourage professional progression.

Bibliography

Kay, J. (2020) *Teachers Lacking Motivation: "Try a sexy sideway"*. [Online] Available from: <https://www.tes.com/news/teachers-lacking-motivation-try-sexy-sideway>. [Accessed 10 November 2022].

APPENDIX 1

Academic Writing/Harvard Referencing Tasks 1 & 2 Plan (Free Resource)

Introduction

For this task you are required to read the short blog. This is an example of an academically written piece of work, which demonstrates the conventions to follow when writing in line with the Harvard referencing system used at xxxxxxx College. In addition, the other attachments and website links below will assist you with completing this task to become accustomed to writing academically. It is compulsory to do this for the level 4 BTEC Professional Diploma in Pharmacy Clinical Services course you are now completing (applicable to the assignment level work).

- <https://library.bradfordcollege.ac.uk/Referencing>
- <https://leaponline.bolton.ac.uk/My-Academic-Development/My-Writing-Techniques/Referencing/Level-2/Harvard-Referencing.aspx#:~:text=In%20the%20text%20of%20your,year%20of%20publication%20in%20brackets>

Task 1:
After reading the resources provided and short blog included later in the plan, you now need to independently research a topic related to pharmacy/wider healthcare that interests you. Write a short piece of work on your chosen topic (suggested word count 600–700), in accordance with Harvard referencing.

As a minimum for this task, your tutor expects you to include three references from reputable resources excluding Wikipedia. Wikipedia is not deemed as a reputable resource at xxxxxxx College. Use correct in-text citations for information you have paraphrased, (rephrased in your own words) from completing your background research on the chosen topic. Your research needs to be expressed objectively. Note that with assignment work more references are expected.

Example topics:

- Review a current news story centring on healthcare, and explore the applications to your practice or to you. Possible examples include news coverage on COVID-19, a report published on a drug, or a medical condition.
- Explain the dangers of smoking, and how smoking cessation treatments can be used to assist patients.
- Assess an update to a particular piece of legislation or national guidance and reflect on how this impacted your area of work.
- Discuss a drug or medical condition that you are interested in and relate the significance to your pharmacy practice.
- Examine the changing roles of Pharmacy professionals and assess the pertinence to your own pharmacy practice.

These are example topic suggestions, but students have the option to select any relevant topic they would like to independently research in more detail.

Upload task 1 as a word document on Ecordia/Moodle.

Task 2:

After completing task 1, now complete a reflective account on your first academically written piece of work for the level 4 course. The reflective account should embody the following:

- What you found the most enjoyable for this task?
- The relevance to your work and studies?
- Anything new you may have learned/any areas you have improved in after completing this specific task? For instance, in your academic writing style or new knowledge acquired.
- Add in anything else you would like to learn more about or develop further on (detail how you would like to do this)?

- Also, to assist us with quality improvement on the course, please provide any comments in your reflective account on any areas where this task could be improved upon?

Your reflective account (suggested word count 400) needs to be submitted via Ecordia/Moodle after you share the reflective account with your mentor, to complete a professional discussion and reflect on the learning from this task. This is a good opportunity to share task 1 too, so they can see your first piece of academic writing on the course.

The mentor needs to add comments on how the learning will impact the learner in terms of what they have learned, and how the development of academic writing and academic study skills could impact their pharmacy practice!

To help format the reflective account use either the DIEP model of reflection, or ERA cycle or the Gibbs model. Alternatively, you can use a different model for your reflective account.

Top Tips on Writing and Referencing

Remember to double-check your work carefully after taking a short mental break to spot and correct any typos before submitting the work on Ecordia/Moodle.

Another top tip is to refer to the example blog below, and to have open the documents attached including the Pocket Guide/links provided earlier when you come to reference your work. This will assist you when formatting your in-text citations.

Continue using the resources within this task for your own assignment work. This alongside the clinical content in your work is what your course lecturer is assessing your work for. We not only want to develop your clinical skills, but alongside this we endeavour to help you progress with your academic writing skills too.

If you have any questions or would like to seek further clarification on the conventions of academic writing, please get in touch with your course tutor/lecturer. We appreciate this style of writing may be new for some of our students, or you may not have written academically for a while therefore your course tutor can provide valuable support in this area.

Please see the example blog overleaf to help you with structuring your in-text citations and formatting your work.

Example Blog: The importance of social learning theory to my level 3 apprentices, but what if their professional role models turn out to be villains?

Introduction

Harold Shipman is a doctor convicted of murdering 15 patients using morphine injections, although the real number was thought to be 215 patients or more (The Guardian, 2000). Healthcare professionals are trusted members of society, and they can be integral in sculpting apprentices or newly qualified healthcare professionals so they exhibit best practice. The significance of this will be explored in this blog.

Extending this point further it is where social learning theory comes to the forefront within teaching on pharmacy courses, as each trainee pharmacy technician has a workplace mentor and they shadow other senior members of staff which exemplifies vicarious learning (Pajares, 2002). This is imperative for trainees as they need to have a professional role model who embodies the General Pharmaceutical Council (GPhC) standards, and exhibits best practice in their work therefore the student acquires key skills.

With any profession however, there are individuals who are "bad apples". They may display bad practice, so again this needs to be considered. It can be a real concern, as this may lead to the students picking up potentially dangerous practice.

The healthcare sector was rocked by the notorious Harold Shipman case; therefore, healthcare is governed by strict rules and regulations. To help mitigate this risk of having poor professional role models for students, there could be a case for more strict and stringent vetting to be undertaken for workplace mentors. This is to ensure that the trainee is safe, and that their mentor would serve as a good professional role model who the student can turn to for advice and support. As an offshoot to this having a good rapport with the students is essential to ensure that they can feel empowered to voice any concerns they may have about their workplace or staff members they work with. Learning generic good workplace values, skills and etiquette is essential for all students in higher education and further education settings, because these students will then go on to become the future workforce and careers are dynamic. Having a basic set of generic work-related skills is vital. More consideration is being devoted to learning outcomes which support employability (FELTAG, 2012). These are generic and include analytical and adaptable learning capabilities with emphasis placed on areas not just restricted to the curriculum, but for instance on confidence, self-discipline, communication, teamwork, questioning attitudes and reflexivity. It supports self-directed learning, meta-cognition principles, and andragogy which encompasses humanistic, and constructivist principles partly reinforced by the Imperial College London approach (Buitendijk, 2017). The workplace mentor has a part to play in honing apprentice/student work orientated skills.

There are examples of registered pharmacists who have exhibited clear unsafe and poor practice unearthed by an undercover BBC investigation (Lynn, 2013). Prescription-only medicines were being sold to members of the public without a prescription for monetary benefit. This is why it is important for the BTEC tutors/lecturers to be a source of support, and for the curriculum to exemplify GPhC standard 8 for pharmacy professionals, "speak up when they have concerns or when things go wrong" (General Pharmaceutical Council, 2024).

Conclusion

Workplace mentors are instrumental in shaping the future pharmacy workforce. After further research into this area, it reaffirms the importance of rigorous vetting to ensure they can be effective shapers and crafters for impressionable students, and most importantly that they share safe and best practice so the students emulate this. It is vital to assist in ensuring a competent future pharmacy workforce to help address the issues the NHS is currently facing, through effective collaborative working practices in multidisciplinary teams.

Bibliography

Buitendijk, S. (2017) *Innovative Teaching for World Class Learning: Learning and Teaching Strategy*. [Online] Available from: <https://www.imperial.ac.uk/media/imperial-college/about/leadership-and-strategy/vp-education/public/LearningTeachingStrategy.pdf>. [Accessed 05 May 2019].

FELTAG. (2012) *FELTAG Recommendations*. [Online] Available from: <http://feltag.org.uk/wp-content/uploads/2012/01/FELTAG-REPORT-FINAL.pdf>. [Accessed 25 August 2024].

General Pharmaceutical Council. (2024) *Standards for Pharmacy Professionals*. [Online] Available from: <https://www.pharmacyregulation.org/pharmacists/standards-and-guidance-pharmacy-professionals/standards-pharmacy-professionals> [Accessed 24 August 2024].

The Guardian. (2000) *Shipman Found Guilty of Murdering 15 Patients*. [Online] Available from: <https://www.theguardian.com/uk/2000/jan/31/shipman.health5>. [Accessed 05 May 2019].

Lynn, G. (2013) *Pharmacists who sold drugs illegally suspended*. [Online] Available from: <https://www.bbc.co.uk/news/uk-england-london-21062630>. [Accessed 24 August 2024].

Pajares, F. (2002) *Overview of Social Cognitive Theory and of Self-Efficacy*. [Online] Available from: <https://people.wku.edu/richard.miller/banduratheory.pdf>. [Accessed 24 August 2024].

APPENDIX 2

TES Article How to Improve College Students' Academic Writing

<https://www.tes.com/magazine/archived/how-improve-college-students-academic-writing>
> Note that readers must be subscribers to TES to access the article. (Ahmed, 2020)

APPENDIX 3

HEA Fellowship Application Reflective Account

Introduction

In this reflective account I will be analysing my experience in relation to the domains to acquire FHEA status using the Brookfield's lenses. To begin with under the autobiographical lens, this is my second year of active teaching practice in higher education. I am a qualified pharmacist who has undertaken a MPharm (awarded first class honours degree), CAVA award level 3, and last year I completed my level 7 postgraduate diploma in Education and Training (achieved merit level). For this I centred my action research project on literacy skills development, and how to improve academic writing/Harvard referencing for science-based students for the courses I teach on including the higher education Level 4 BTEC Professional Diploma in Pharmacy Clinical Services (A1). The action research project attained an 82 per cent mark, and derived progression in this area for students where all made headway in advancing literacy skills together with academic writing proficiency. It stimulated conversations from students on further refinements in this area. A significant improvement in literacy skills was achieved. I used reflective accounts to help students identify where they could develop, and to take charge of their learning. In the student reflective accounts, I inserted a quality assurance mechanism, where I asked the students what worked well on the task and if there was anything that could be improved upon. Enabling the student voice to provide feedback on the course and tasks is an effective quality assurance tool on learning resources and should be embedded wherever possible on courses. Evaluating student feedback provided an ample opportunity to reflect from the student perspective and assists in having a more democratic approach to learning. This project was published in TES, March 2020, and it was instrumental in making enrichments to the task for the following year (discussed later more intricately) (A5 and V3).

Disseminating further under the self-analysis lens, to keep my knowledge and skills current I locum as a pharmacist. I have worked for NHS 111 to support patients, or their representatives who call NHS 111. Queries I receive from the public could pertain to medicines information requests or could be related to toxic ingestion. My recent clinical experience lends to the feedback I provide to my students, and it helps me connect the taught knowledge to clinical practice (K1). Another key component to my clinical teaching is attending conferences and NHS training events. Last year I attended the national Pharmacy conference, where I was able to attend workshops to support my CPD needs. One of the workshops was on the changing structures within the NHS (K1 and A5), and I used this learning as a base for the unit 4 lesson revisions on NHS structures and clinical ethics. I rewrote the lessons to incorporate the new advances, and considered how this impacts clinical governance. I ruminated on how to make these lessons both applicable to primary and secondary care settings for pharmacy technicians working in different settings (A1, V2, V3 and V4). After reflecting on the workshop, and feedback from my course lead I designed the tasks so there was an ethical scenario for primary care and secondary care too. One ethical scenario was predicated in community pharmacy about a young female minor requesting emergency hormonal contraception (EHC) accompanied by a much older man (this task allowed for those situated in primary care to consider safeguarding elements) (V2).

The second ethical scenario created was set for the students working in a GP setting. Students were asked how to respond when a mother called asking, "What are the Microgynon tablets I've found in my 15-year-old daughters' room for"? The task assessed how students would deal with medicines information requests coupled with parental concerns, and reflect keenly on how data protection principles and the Gillick Competence and Fraser Guidelines would factor in to their responses to inform the steps they would take if presented with a similar situation in practice.

To incorporate secondary care, I designed a final ethical scenario to assess how the students would respond if a patient on a mental health ward requested information about lithium side effects from a pharmacy technician, who then chose to withhold the information due to concerns that the patient may not adhere with their medication. Would this be morally acceptable? Can consent to treatment be valid in this situation if the patient isn't abreast of all the information? Using my previous experience working in healthcare settings (autobiographical lens), coupled with the knowledge gained (theoretical perspective) from attending the workshop it helped me prepare content encompassing challenging ethical scenarios which every student on the course could relate to, and could explore working practices in varied healthcare settings. There is a multitude of clinical and ethical considerations that registered Pharmacy professionals come across in their day-to-day work. By providing scenarios in different settings on a variety of possible situations it helps cultivate important clinical reasoning skills and affords opportunities for the students to review how clinical ethics impact everyday practice. During the pandemic and pre-pandemic eras healthcare professionals were faced with situations and scenarios, where ethics played a huge part in fair and equitable clinical service provision in both primary and secondary care. Advancing knowledge and skills in clinical ethics is fundamental to healthcare disciplines.

Furthermore, I delivered training based on patient monitoring case studies for delegates attending an NHS training event. It demonstrated how detailed assessments on case studies help to bolster clinical skills acquisition for pharmacy technicians. The event was hosted by Health Education England (V4), and it helped foster a good working relationship between our teaching team and representatives from key stakeholders.

Reflecting more keenly under the theoretical lens strategies employed in my teaching pedagogy include situational learning theory. It advocates the benefits attached to working and learning to gain professional skills from the periphery. Over time more knowledge is gained, and skills are nurtured to enable greater participation in the community of practice. My students on the level 4 course share features with this, where they have a mentor in the workplace and other colleagues they can turn to for support. The course entails clinical pharmacy knowledge and motivates the students to augment their clinical analytical skillsets developing clinical skills necessary for the workplace (Northern Illinois University Centre for Innovative Teaching and Learning, 2012). A pedagogical approach of case study learning is used to assess a wide breath of clinical skills, and retention of clinical knowledge appropriate to practice (A2). All the students work in a pharmacy setting; they have an allocated mentor and a course tutor who is a registered Pharmacy professional. A central dogma to my teaching is to provide context to the clinical learning. It allows for meaningful attainment of knowledge and skills, which can be used by the students to tackle clinical issues related to patient care. Wenger and Lave are influential backers of learning to be achieved in this manner (Kurt, 2021).

The courses I teach on are delivered online and the learning resources are designed to be inclusive and transferable between different pharmacy settings, irrespective of whether the students are based in a community, hospital, GP, Primary Care Network (PCN) or Ministry of Defence (MOD) setting. For any working professional careers are ever evolving. Having both a broad and bespoke approach to course delivery is key for any learner who may decide to move between settings, and to support them in their present chosen field. The tasks I devise and lessons I have authored such as on Microbiology, Pain and Respiratory disorders have been constructed in a manner which reflects best practice and supports active clinical acumen skills acquirement.

The learning is self-directed and independent, but allows a sense of a learning community to flourish. A Telegram support group for students has been established where learning, and conversations about learning to support their own personal metacognition occur frequently (A4, K3, K4 and V4). It is wonderful to see how the learners share best practice with each other, especially with the student contributions in online lessons. In the Microbiology lesson I asked the students to discuss the MRSA (methicillin-resistant *Staphylococcus aureus*) decolonisation protocols they have in their area of work, and it facilitated a great interactive conversation about the different options used. They discussed which groups this is advised for in their settings. By them sharing their own protocols it enabled for best practice to be shared in an inclusive manner and prompted additional student

Appendix 3

Table 2. A Table to Show Student Feedback on How the Microbiology Lesson Could Be Further Improved

1	Anonymous	A longer lesson?
2	Anonymous	Possibly signposting to some useful sources of information, websites etc.
3	Anonymous	I like the way the lesson was made relevant to practice, so apologies this is not an improvement – but just noticing something that was fab
4	Anonymous	It couldn't be, it was great.
5	Anonymous	More info on specific treatments (drugs) for types of micro-organisms
6	Anonymous	More quizzes!

comments such as "that it would be a great CPD opportunity for them to learn more about other MRSA decolonisation protocols" (K3 and V1).

Within teaching delivery, it is imperative to muse on how effective the teaching is. Therefore, for the online lessons I concocted a Microsoft Teams form, which I asked the students to complete online to gauge how they rated the lesson and suggest possible future adjustments (gaining further insight through the student point of view). Learning analytics is essential to achieving quality assurance (Johnson et al., 2016). Below are excerpts of online student feedback on the Microbiology lesson, and Table 2 depicts how the students envisioned the lesson could be further enriched:

> "I enjoyed the quiz the most as it reassures you that you have learnt something new."
>
> "Finding out about different types of microorganisms and having examples provided to put it into context."
>
> "I found it very informative and it was paced very well."

After reviewing this I updated the Microbiology online lesson to add resources, which students could be signposted to in order to shore up their learning, and to lengthen the quiz as this makes the lesson more interactive. Effective quality assurance measures help accomplish the ambition of continually refining the course. This is useful in ensuring the student voice is heard using a digital platform with the use of learning analytics amongst other methods to inform course improvements (Ferrell et al., 2018). To promote reflective learning practice in the student reviews, I asked about any future learning interests after attending this online lesson. Below is a direct quote from a student on how they took the learning from the Microbiology lesson to identify what they needed to do next to cement their learning (A1, A2, K2, K3, K4, K5, K6):

> I would like to refresh some more of my microbiology as it is not an area I feel comfortable with knowledge wise.

A Microsoft Teams channel has been created where not only are the online lessons delivered, but regular workshops are held to embolden the students to have another platform to communicate with one another and share best practice. This allows the course tutors to hold drop-in sessions with the students to discuss any concerns/questions, or anxieties they may have in relation to the course. Tutorial support is available on the phone, and via WhatsApp too making the teaching staff as accessible as possible (A4 and K4).

Alongside this the teaching embraces elements of social development theory, where students have a more active role in their learning rather than the view of the instructionist model of learning (teacher-centric). The students are motivated to draw on their practical experience and share best practice with their tutors/lecturers and fellow students. It permits a supportive learning community to prosper and improves their clinical pharmacy practice (V1). This is like the "more knowledgeable other" where the students learn from each other, their course tutor, and their workplace mentor as well (Learning Theories, 2020a).

Reflecting further under the theoretical vantage point cognitivist elements are assimilated too. Between units 2 and 3 connections are highlighted, and links are established with previous learning. In unit 2 adverse drug reactions and therapeutic drug monitoring are considered in a detailed manner, then in the unit 3 assignment work this is revisited where drug factors and concepts such as evidence-based medicine in relation to medication choices are surveyed. By reassessing an important area of learning repeatedly, as put forward in the spiral curriculum ethos (branching from cognitivism) by authors such as Bruner (n.d., cited in Johnston 2012), it showcases how learning theories such as the spiral curriculum are integral to the learning for students enrolled on healthcare courses/science disciplines (A1). The learners are active information constructors making more definitive links between units, and simultaneously reinforcing how this connects to wider clinical pharmacy service provision in the workplace (Learning Theories, 2020b) (K3).

With the academic writing/Harvard referencing task I kept in mind that we have learners, who learn best in different ways therefore this is taught interactively as part of the mandatory induction lesson. Online resources are provided and for more visual learners they have the recorded lesson to refer to exploiting both the visual and auditory memory capacities in the brain. I strongly recommend that referencing should be taught at the start of the course (it's a skill which takes time to develop) and should be revisited thereafter (Lamptey and Atta-Obeng, 2012) (K2 and V3).

I attempt to entrench reflective practice wherever possible by establishing reflective learning. Elements of heutagogy and andragogy are used to challenge students to examine where they sit at presently, and what they need to do to develop to reach the next level/goalpost (A2 and K2). The use of constructivism and humanism elements amongst other learning theories to encourage lifelong self-determined learning is endorsed in literature (Blashke and Hase, 2016).

This reflective component to learning is promoted when the students complete the reflective account in the academic writing/Harvard referencing task, at the end of each unit evaluation, and as part of the reflective diary for the specialist project (a local research project to be completed in their work setting). The reflective diary and reflective accounts help to identify any challenges that students have faced and expand on strategies implemented to overcome the identified issues. In particular COVID-19 has led to obstacles in data collation for their specialist research projects, and when there were shortages of PPE Pharmacy staff had very limited patient and peer contact. Many were redeployed to other areas such as the vaccination hubs, and so the teaching team collectively agreed to be lenient with target dates under these exceptional circumstances. Moreover, on numerous occasions the advice I have provided on student research projects is to use electronic data wherever possible, and make sure patient identifiable information is anonymised. This helps make their projects more pandemic proof and conforms to data protection guidelines (K5).

Another positive aspect of the reflective account that I set for the academic writing/referencing task (K4) is that it requested the students to include any ways that the task itself could be improved upon (a key element to my published research project), which was shared in Chapter 7 of the book. The published article can be accessed in the website link in Appendix 2. Thus, last year I updated the task to take on board the student feedback provided. Some students said, "a pre-set list of topics would help", and others said "I liked that the task was so open and could choose what to write about". I merged both ideas together and provided some examples, although left the option to research something completely independent (K5).

Having an ethos within the course where lessons are updated and reviewed at regular intervals through deep introspection, via multiple perspectives such as the self-critical lens, peer lens, theoretical lens, and student viewpoint is key to propelling upgrades forward to achieve a better learner experience. One of the points from the Pearson external verification report was to encourage improvements in relation to academic writing. As an outcome the academic/Harvard referencing task came to fruition. After I reviewed this update by examining these key perspectives, I then as part of our stringent in-house quality assurance measures distributed this to the course lead, and the rest of the teaching team to see if any other changes were required (A2, K2, K3, K5, K6, V1). By doing this it allowed me to reflect on valuable peer feedback to analyse this more thoroughly (peer angle). The course lead is a keen advocate of quality assurance for the course learning materials and resources. Even though this is a course based on a science discipline by championing literacy skills development, and academic writing this promotes adherence to evidence-based practice. It allows for these values to be encouraged in the practice of our students on the course. Making this link between higher education, and self-directed study related to a wider context allows for multi-layered learning to take place (V4). It motivates the students to gain deep self-analysis on how they best learn and helps them fulfil the reflective component in lifelong learning as registered pharmacy professionals (GPhC, 2024).

Appendix 3

It is key to make habitual periodic deep reflections for healthcare professionals, as when mistakes happen it assists in completing a root cause analysis. This supports clinical governance measures which are at the heart of NHS working practices, so others can learn by sharing learning from critical incidents with the wider team including with other departments. This encourages more joined-up working in MDTs (multidisciplinary teams). The tasks with reflective components allow the students to enhance this particular skill set and portrays how pharmacy professionals are working towards the NHS constitutional values (V4).

As part of my teaching remit, I must assess formative and summative assignments. Such formative assessments include assessing COVID-19 and flu contingency plans (a task for the Microbiology lesson introduced earlier). Many of our students have used this opportunity to create a workplace policy for either flu, or COVID-19 that their workplace managers have then decided to use in their hospital and community pharmacy departments. It's brilliant to see the gains and positives that the learning on this course helps to achieve. Such tasks centring on situated learning theory blended with constructivism facets help bring about improvements in clinical research skills and assists learning to reflect what happens at the foundation levels in clinical settings to produce progressions in clinical pharmacy service operations (A2 and V4). See below excerpts of feedback which show how I use the concept of "feedforward" as coined by Race (2007) to help assist with student progression (A3).

This is a very professional-looking policy that you have developed. Well done!

Note that with influenza type A, it can undergo mutations and antigenic drift in the HA (haemagglutinin) or neuraminidase (NA) genes. The change or changes at these sites means antibodies may no longer be effective, and the defences of the immune system can be evaded resulting in a potential pandemic.

Sound recommendations made in your policy to help prevent the spread of the flu virus, supporting effective infection control measures.

Above is an example of feedback constructed for a formative task I assessed on a flu contingency plan created by a student. The student had considered workplace contingency planning and hygiene measures in depth but did not elaborate in a detailed manner on how flu pandemics may emerge.

It was touched on briefly but it could have been expanded on in the policy created, so I used detailed feedback as above to boost their learning (A3).

To make the learning as inclusive as possible within the enrolment forms there is a section on specific learning needs and disabilities (SpLDs). On a few occasions I have had to forward details to our team that evaluates and diagnoses SpLDs. By taking on board the diagnostic recommendations, I have adapted lessons/learning to include videos for instance within the Microbiology, Pain and Harvard referencing lessons. Students that have dyslexia have preferred this mode of learning. For other students who have anxiety especially when it comes to writing assignments at level 4, I have amended my teaching style to deliver mini workshops using Microsoft Teams or have completed tutorials over the telephone. Just by going through the machinations involved in Harvard referencing, this supports students with additional learning needs to improve in their assignment work and grow in confidence in academic writing. It helps ensure that none of our students are disadvantaged, and where appropriate extensions have been agreed to provide extra time for affected students. The course does not discriminate against anyone and is eligible to all pharmacy technicians that are registered with the GPhC, and for anyone that has a disability such as a visual impairment I have adapted the resources so a bigger font size is used. Small adaptations like this and advising the student to complete work in a larger font size with an agreed extension helps assure that we comply with the Equality Act, 2010 (V1 and V2).

Conclusion

As promoted in humanism metacognition is based on the premise that all individuals can be effective learners, if they know how to learn. This is where a deep reflection proves essential for tangible learning to be attained (Huitt, 2009). My practice as a dual professional (a Pharmacist and a Lecturer) allows me to challenge my students to achieve deeper learning, where I share my experiences with them to illustrate how clinical pharmacy provision can be modified to improve patient care in many different workstreams (to consider that there may be more than one appropriate option). Teaching workshops for NHS/HEE events means that I have connections with NHS organisations. Strong links with key stakeholders is fundamental to growing the reputation of HE courses like this. As part of my studies I have completed a MPharm (where I have learned in depth clinical knowledge on the area of pharmacokinetics, anatomy, and pharmacology). My own learning within HE coupled with my post-registration experience has allowed me to craft tasks, and student learning resources founded in learning theories such as situated learning theory and constructivism. By mixing different learning theories with clinical content from my own Pharmacy practice especially that stemming from my work at NHS 111, it helped me to come up with learning activities that solidifies meaningful learning to take place for the students. My action research project discussed in Chapter 7 of the book, allowed me to sharpen my teaching skills to not only convey the significance of evidence-based research, but to augment the academic writing skills of my students. I hope to continue to advance in my teaching practice to develop the learning experience of my HE students.

As part of my teaching practice, I have recently been promoted to Course Revisions Lead for the course I teach on, and the pandemic was a difficult time to undertake a new set of responsibilities at work. After a further six months had lapsed I was promoted to "Joint Pharmacy Professional Development Lead". I used the tool of reflection to think about how I could ensure the peer perspective, and student vantage points could be gauged when renovating course materials. As an unexpected and welcome outcome of this my reflective account was published in the Impact Journal, and this is included in Chapter 2. In the reflective account in the second chapter I wanted to share how issues in teaching practice can be overcome through collaboration and reflection. I have used the Brookfield's model again, because over the other reflective account models I have used I find that this is the model that allows a more rounded explication through exploration of key ideas and events related to teaching practice under multiple angles to capture deeper insight.

Bibliography

Blashke, L. M., and Hase, S. (2016) Chapter 2: A Holistic Framework for Creating Twenty-First Century Self-Determined Learners. In B. Gros, Kinshuk., and M. Maina (eds), *The Future of Ubiquitous Learning Designs for Emerging Pedagogies*. Berlin: Springer-Verlag, pp. 25–40.

Ferrell, G., Smith, R., and Knight, S. (2018) *Designing Learning and Assessment in a Digital Age*. [Online] Available from : <https://www.jisc.ac.uk/guides/designing-learning-and-assessment-in-a-digital-age>. <https://www.jisc.ac.uk/full-guide/designing-learning-and-assessment-in-a-digital-age>. [Accessed 24 August 2024].

GPhC. (2024) *Standards for Pharmacy Professionals*. [Online] Available from: <https://www.pharmacyregulation.org/pharmacists/standards-and-guidance-pharmacy-professionals/standards-pharmacy-professionals>. [Accessed 24 August 2024].

Huitt, W. (2009) *Humanism and Open Education*. [Online] Available from: <https://www.edpsycinteractive.org/topics/affect/humed.html>. [Accessed 12 April 2023].

Johnston, H. (2012) *The Spiral Curriculum*. [Online] Available from: <https://files.eric.ed.gov/fulltext/ED538282.pdf>. [Accessed 31 May 2021].

Johnson, L., Adams Becker, S., Cummins, M., Estrada, V., Freeman, A., and Hall, C. (2016) *NMC: Horizon Report 2016 Higher Education Edition*. Austin, TX: The New Media Consortium.

Kurt, S. (2021) *Situated Learning Theory*. [Online] Available from: <https://educationaltechnology.net/situated-learning-theory/>. [Accessed 31 May 2021].

Lamptey, R. B., and Atta-Obeng, H. (2012) Challenges with Reference Citations among Postgraduate Students at the Kwame Nkrumah University of Science and Technology Kumasi Ghana. *Journal of Science and Technology*, 32(3), pp. 69–80.

Learning Theories. (2020a) *Social Development Theory (Vygotsky)*. [Online] Available from: <https://learning-theories.com/>. [Accessed 25 August 2024].

Learning Theories. (2020b) *Constructivism*. [Online] Available from: <https://learning-theories.com/>. [Accessed 25 August 2024].

Appendix 3

Northern Illinois University, Center for Innovative Teaching and Learning. (2012) *Situated Learning*. [Online] Available from: <https://www.niu.edu/citl/resources/guides/instructional-guide>. [Accessed 17 June 2021].

Race, P. (2007) *The Lecturer's Toolkit*. 3rd edn. Oxon: Routledge.

APPENDIX 4

ITTECF

The full list of the standards can be viewed by visiting the following link: <https://www.gov.uk/government/publications/initial-teacher-training-and-early-career-framework>
(DFE, 2024)

APPENDIX 5

ETF Professional Standards for Teachers and Trainers

These can be viewed in full by visiting the following website:
<https://set.et-foundation.co.uk/your-career/the-professional-standards/the-20-professional-standards-to-enhance-your-practice/>
(ETF, 2022)

APPENDIX 6

Global Framework of Professional Teaching Standards from the Joint EI/UNESCO

These can be viewed in full by visiting the following website (scroll down to access the file):
<https://www.ei-ie.org/en/item/25734:global-framework-of-professional-teaching-standards#:~:text=The%20joint%20Education%20International%2F%20UNESCO%20framework%20on%20the,Development%20and%20specifically%20Sustainable%20Development%20Goal%204%20%28SDG4%29>.

(Education International and UNESCO, 2022)

www.ingramcontent.com/pod-product-compliance
Ingram Content Group UK Ltd.
Pitfield, Milton Keynes, MK11 3LW, UK
UKHW021311180426
11947UKWH00015B/1153